Overcoming

By
Andrel Harris

Library of Congress Cataloging – in- Publication Data has been applied for.

Paperback ISBN: 978-1-7373494-3-3
eBook ISBN: 978-1-7373494-4-0

PRINTED IN THE UNITED STATES OF AMERICA.

Editing & Typesetting by: Carla M. Dean, U Can Mark My Word
Published by: Pen Legacy Publishing
Book cover design by: NBM Global

FIRST EDITION

TABLE OF CONTENTS

Overcoming

Chapter 1

Overcoming Being a
Product of Your Environment

You come here earthbound without an option to choose your environment. In life, there are things we have control over and things we have no control over. One cannot control when or where they are born, the family they are born into, who their parents are, and how their parents raise them. Our parents and families were already chosen for us. There was no control on our part in the creation of our existence.

You were chosen to come at the time you came to live out your soul's purpose. There are mentions that some souls never have human experiences. It is noted that at some point, physical experience no longer serves the soul's awareness, and, therefore, the soul chooses to learn in a nonphysical realm. The reality for you is that you are here; you are aware.

Here we are as souls, molding our personalities of physical form. Earth has now become our new home. We've come here pure and transparent, quickly adapting to the frequency of our surrounding reality.

THE HAND YOU WERE DEALT

"We cannot change the cards we are dealt, just how we play the hand."

Randy Bausch

The molding of who we have become has a lot to do with our upbringing—heavily influenced by beliefs, values, and culture. There are two ways you can deal with the hand you were dealt: You can be bitter, blaming the hand dealt to you, and fold. Or you can do the best you can with it.

People who are bitter about the hand they have been dealt tend to blame their problems on everyone else. Maybe it's the fault of the single mom, absent father, or drug-addicted, abusive parent. If this is true for you, you have to decide right now that you will not allow these circumstances to cause you to live a life of torment.

Then we have the people who do the best with the hand they were dealt and thrive in life. There are countless success stories of people who were dealt a bad hand in life but ended up overcoming the odds and making something great out of something that seemed insignificant. Personally, I love to indulge in rags-to-riches stories. The transformation that occurs in these stories allows me to see what is possible, and from there, I pull a great deal of energy to push through.

Being a product of your environment can be good or bad. Your environment consists of more than your parents or family. It also consists of the era in which you grew up. Growing up in a weak environment or experiencing a void at home can result in a person venturing out to seek their identity. It is why some young children turn to gangs. The lack of guidance can take you down the wrong path. You can't help the environment you grew up in, but most likely, you are the way you are because of it.

This reminds me of my sister and me. We were raised in two different households and had different outlooks on life. I grew up in a more structured household environment , whereas she didn't. My mother was seventeen when she had me, and one year later, she gave birth to my sister. We have different fathers, so my early years were spent between two households, my father's parents and my mom and stepfather.

I lived in New York for a short period of time with my mother and witnessed so much, from different cultures to violence and struggle. This was in the 1980s at the height of the crack epidemic, and in New York, it was a prevailing problem especially in African American communities. So, early on I watched my mom and stepfather have parties and get high with their friends. I didn't think too much of it because I was still young. This was the environment I was exposed to, but even then, I intuitively knew that there was more to life. Despite these circumstances, my mom and stepfather made sure to provide our basic needs. There were times that Christmas missed us, and I wondered why Santa never came. That was heartbreaking as a child. However, as I grew older, I realized that they just didn't have the money to spend on Christmas presents.

There was one Christmas holiday that we were looking forward to. We had gotten the opportunity to pick out a few toys, and my mom had some gifts wrapped up behind the sofa. We had just returned to New York after being in North Carolina, only to find that our apartment was burglarized, and they took everything! We had to make the best of what we had which was each other.

Conversely, there was another environment that I got to experience and grew to love. I was around six years old when I decided to move in with my paternal grandparents in North Carolina. All I could remember at that time was how calm and peaceful the environment was and how they spoiled me. Holidays were filled with love and gifts. I was the first grandchild my grandmother had, so that explains me getting whatever I wanted. This environment was wholly opposite to living in New York. My sister continued to live with my mom and her dad for a while before moving to North Carolina and living with my maternal grandmother. My maternal grandmother had a house full – from aunts to uncles to cousins. She just took everyone in and did the best she could to care for them.

I was raised with a different set of values instilled in me. I was able to evaluate what was important and what wasn't. Observing the world around me, I craved all that life had to offer. I would say that I had a strong guidance system and was able to decipher what was best for me. As far as my sister, I believe that not having a family structure as solid as mine led to her being influenced by the outside world. Sometimes peers can influence your life. If the right knowledge isn't instilled in us, we may ask the world, "Who am I?" — instead of receiving deposits from those positive influences in your life — which can lead down a troublesome road full of bad decision making. Our lives currently are very different, and I believe it is due to what we were exposed to at a young age. These were the hands that we were dealt, and we played them the best we knew how.

So, I would ask, does your environment have an effect on your life? Do you believe your life would have turned out differently if you were raised another way?

Being that you cannot change your upbringing, choosing to embrace what has been engrained in you and making the necessary changes for a different outcome will require some mental and emotional toughness. You are going to have to unlearn some things, check your emotions, and understand that where you are from and how you were raised doesn't have to dictate where you are headed and how far you can go now.

It doesn't matter where you come from or how bad you think your past was, you are the only one who can stop you from achieving anything more than you desire. If you are constantly in an environment where you are surrounded by pessimistic, small minded, or fear-based people, it is bound to impact your dreams, therefore, slowing down your progression. For me, it was quite simple. I wanted to surround myself with confident, optimistic, and insanely ambitious people. I knew that this type of environment would influence me to believe in the possibility of my own visions and have enough confidence to follow them through. When I found my tribe, suddenly my view of the world expanded, and there were no limits. I was challenged to be more, and as a result, I pushed myself and thrived. I was happy with who I was becoming. Who you choose to spend the majority of your time with will determine the path you will end up taking, and their influence will ripple throughout all aspects of your life.

A few things to consider if you're wanting to overcome being a product of your environment:

- Change your environment. Observe people who have the lifestyle you wish to adopt. Look at their habits and surroundings. Put yourself in the right rooms or relocate, if necessary.

- Seek knowledge. Never stop learning. Take a course, read books, or hire mentors for each area of your life you would like to change.

- Connect to a higher power. Tap into that which you believe in and ask for guidance and strength.

- Seek counseling. If you were raised in a traumatic environment, reach out to talk with a therapist.

At this very moment, you can decide to tap into the power within you and change the trajectory of your path if it is unpleasing. Your life was chosen for you; what you do with the hand you were dealt is ultimately up to you.

"Surround yourself with dreamers and doers, the believers and thinkers, but most of all, surround yourself with those who see greatness within you, even when you don't see it yourself."

— *Steve Jobs*

Chapter 2
Overcoming the Transition

Life transitions can be exciting for some while frightening for others. New chapters are full of unknowns and what-ifs. Yet, whether we are fully prepared or not, change is inevitable. I encourage you to think deeper than the reality surface. You are here to learn, and while on your journey, you will encounter setbacks. However, you will also have successes.

There is a Buddhist concept that I found to be quite interesting called the "Wheel of Life," which is a visual depiction of the Buddhists' view of our existence as a cycle of life, death, rebirth, and "suffering." The Buddhists believed this recurring cycle is the very essence of life. This philosophy caused me to ponder a bit. If we want to have a meaningful life full of purpose and joy, we must learn to adapt to the constant state of change that turns the wheel of life.

Resisting transitions and change will only interrupt the flow of abundance into our lives, altering the natural rhythm. At some point, we have to be open to allowing new frequencies to create shifts in our lives so that we can continue to grow and evolve. Many of us find it difficult to evolve because of our inability to let go of the way things used to be. We hold on to old habits, thought patterns, and even situationships, not realizing it is blocking us from receiving the blessings that await us in the future.

When I moved away from Elizabeth City, North Carolina, I was ready for change. I was ready to bid adieu to an old familiar way of being. I was ready to experience a new environment, embark upon new opportunities, and meet new people. Even though I felt sentimental as I said my goodbyes, I was also anxious about what could be in store for me. What seemed like an ending was actually a new beginning. I organized a plan of action and started to see things slowly manifest. I would like to note that I could already see myself possession of what I wanted prior to achieving my goals.

Here I was in a new city and ready for my fresh beginning. It took me a while to get used to a bigger city. I was okay with the traffic, but there weren't any GPS navigation systems during that time. We had handwritten directions from someone who already knew the way. We also had maps and payphones. So, whenever we got lost, we pulled over at a gas station to ask for directions or make a phone call. Sometimes I sit and think about how much technology has evolved and has made driving so much easier. I remember it taking an hour to get from my cousin's house back to where I was staying. It was because I was driving around in circles. But other than getting lost, I was excited to start creating a new chapter.

I landed my first job at a UPS call center, making more money than I had been making. I still remember the days of working my first job at McDonald's for minimum wage in North Carolina. That job, even with low pay, was exciting because it was my first job. I was just happy to make my own money, and I enjoyed working with classmates. We created many pleasant memories. I remember one crazy experience when I thought I was going to freeze to death—literally. I went into the walk-in freezer to get something we had run out of, and when the door closed behind me, I was locked in. I remember banging and yelling for help to the top of my lungs for what felt like an eternity. I mean, my hands were red and hurting from the banging. Finally, help came.

When I needed more pay, I would drive to the beach about forty-five minutes away. Before I moved, my last job in Elizabeth City was at Food Lion in Nags Head, North Carolina. The pay was about $7.00/hour. I didn't mind working in order to get the things I wanted. I always kept a job once I reached the age where I could work. As I reminisce about this time, I find it a little hilarious that I wanted to transfer my Food Lion job from Nags Head to Greensboro, North Carolina. I still remember telling my aunt, who lived in Greensboro, that I wanted to transfer, and I wanted her to get a few applications for me. I remember her saying I could find another job somewhere else. I had to get out of the mindset of just having those types of jobs, and I'm glad I listened.

Greensboro provided more job opportunities and better pay; this made the transition even more exciting. I was excited about working at the call center because we didn't have those types of jobs. I was used to standing on my feet for long hours and being physically drained by the end of the workday. I thought nothing of it because it provided for the lifestyle that I wanted at the time. Working at the UPS call center was a whole different ballgame. It was more of a professional setting, and I thought having my own cubicle was the best thing. As I toured the building during orientation, I was highly satisfied with starting the job. I no longer had to stand for hours; now, I could sit down all day while talking on the phone and typing data into a computer. Talk about being grateful; I was elated! Not to mention they had an onsite cafeteria. This was perfect for me.

Not only did I enjoy this new line of work, but I was also meeting new friends. Other than my two aunts and a few cousins, I didn't know anyone else here. The group of people whom I trained with became my first set of friends. They would invite me out to various activities and parties. Back then, there were a lot of house parties. I remember a coach from the job used to throw parties all the time. This one night, a couple of the girls from the class decided to meet up and go. We partied so hard that a few work buddies had to end up driving us home because we were too intoxicated to drive our cars. Everyone decided to stay over at my house until the next day. It was good clean fun with great people in a great environment.

Fast-forward a couple of years later, circa 2003. I wanted to pursue my passion of becoming a cosmetologist. This was also another exciting time for me because I could now do hair legally. Here's how I discovered my talent. When I moved from New York to live with my grandmother, everything seemed to be going well. Everything except for my hair! You see, my mother always did me and my sister's hair, and she was very good at it. My grandmother, on the other hand, was not.

I remember when I first arrived to live with my grandmother, one of the first things she said was, "We got to get those braids out of your head." She didn't like them at all. This reminded me of an old movie called *Crooklyn*. In that film, the young girl lived with her mother in New York but went down south to stay with her relatives. They didn't care too much for her braids, so they made her take them out.

My grandmother would often send me to the beauty salon or have one of my aunts put a curly kit in my hair. Back then, people would tease you for having it, so I told myself that I had to make something work. I couldn't go to school with my hair looking a mess. Luckily, I had the reversible curly kit that I could wear straight. One day, while looking through old photo albums, I came across a picture of my aunt, who was my grandmother's daughter. In the picture, she had two ponytails sticking straight out from her head—similar to two horns! I immediately took action. Little did I know, it was the start of something great. As I sat in my room, I would practice all sorts of styles and experiment with different products. The way my thought process worked, I refused to leave my room until my hair was styled and left no reason for it to be redone. And guess what? It worked!

Well, this was also my first experience with entrepreneurship. Not legally, but I was determined to work my craft. I began doing family members' and close friends' hair. I did hair for holidays and other occasions.

One day, my best friend, cousin, and I had an idea to start a beauty salon in the garage at my house. We had curated all the details, designated each person with a specific job task, and even had a nail menu. I had just gotten a new computer that Christmas, so we were able to print up some flyers with prices. The next thing we had to come up with was a name, which was simple. We used the name of our favorite boy group at that time: Another Bad Creation. So, there it was: Another Bad Creation Beauty Salon. Looking back on this name, it was quite hilarious. Clearly, we weren't thinking, because who would want a bad creation, let alone another one? Nonetheless, we were excited about our new endeavor.

The craziest thing about this is we were so determined to make this happen that we presented our plan to my grandmother. We asked her if we could convert the garage into a salon. Her response was, "Y'all are going to jail. You don't have a license the first." We begged her and tried to make sense of it all, but it didn't work. At this point, we were back to square one. Sadly, that ended there, but I continued doing hair for my friends and family. I created a price list for services and even charged my friends to use my hair products. They got clever, though. As soon as I walked out of my bedroom, they would hurry and sneak into my products. I still laugh when I think back on that time.

I looked at this as a blessing in disguise. Had my grandmother known how to do hair, there's no telling when or if I would have discovered my talent. All of us who had the idea of running a salon back then went on to cosmetology school. One of them has a salon located in Elizabeth City, North Carolina. As for me, I still have dreams of opening up my own salon/spa in the near future. I plan to be the owner of the salon and not a worker.

I soon realized being a stylist is a very demanding job. When women want their hair done, they want it done. They couldn't care less about anything other than you keeping their appointment. This is also a linear line of work. If you don't work, you don't get paid. My mindset has shifted from being a stylist to owning a business; that way, I can have others working for me. Since I still love the art of hairstyling, I will get a private suite so I can do hair periodically. I already have a name in mind and a vision for the salon/spa.

Sometimes we plan for things to go one way, but they end up going totally in the opposite direction. This is perfectly fine. Sometimes your experiences in life will change your path to things more to your liking, to more of what feels right, or to more of what makes the most sense. Don't allow overthinking or the fear of the unknown to stop you from doing what you want to do.

Plenty of times, I have read stories of people who said

they wouldn't be who and what they are today if they had never done XYZ. These transitional periods are what make us stronger and wiser. Think about it for a second—if you resist the transition, you will have regrets about the chances you didn't take.

I happily embraced the next phase in life—making more money, pursuing my passion, and meeting new people. I went from working a minimum wage job to making more money at a call center. I went from doing hair in a kitchen to becoming a licensed cosmetologist. Did I have some trying moments? Absolutely! But I also became a better person, and I look forward to moving into the new phases, knowing that everything somehow works together for my highest and best good. Everything during this early transition phase taught me that a definite plan backed by having a burning desire leads to fulfillment.

When transitioning into new chapters in your life, it's also important to hold on to past gems, such as memories and valuable life lessons. All of this necessitates the need for coping mechanisms that will enable you to make a smooth transition from your past to a new era that awaits you. As you move through the passage of change, leave the pain and bad memories of the past behind. You don't want this to hinder you. Don't hold on to grudges. I know it can be hard; I still struggle with this myself. But, at some point, we have to let it go. I shared my early transitions regarding moving away, adapting to a new environment, and embracing new opportunities. Your transitions may be different. But wherever you are, leave with a sense of gratitude and let go of any emotional baggage. Carry faith with your wisdom. Every experience that we have happens for a reason; it all works together for your evolution. Get clear about your vision and set new goals. Get excited about having a fresh start—a do-over where you are armed with wisdom from your past experiences.

"There will come a time when you believe everything is finished. That will be the beginning."

~ Unknown

Chapter 3
Overcoming Setbacks

Grief Setbacks

Anyone who wants to achieve anything in life will suffer from some setbacks on their way. Setbacks are a part of life for all of us. Sometimes when we think we're ready to unleash on the world, the universe shows us it has other plans. One of my first setbacks in life was a blow.

My life seemed to be going pretty well. I was in a new city, making more money, and meeting new people. After experiencing much success during this chapter of my life, my world came crumbling down on October 28, 2003. My first love, my high school sweetheart, passed away. I still remember receiving that phone call in the wee hours of the morning.

It was raining this particular night, and the house phone rang, jolting me out of my sleep. I remember picking up the phone in a state of confusion, and I could hear a voice saying, "Andrel, wake up. Andrel, wake up."

I knew something bad had happened.

"Who is it?" I kept asking.

"It's Brian," his aunt said. "He's gone."

At that moment, I felt as though my heart had been ripped out of my chest. There was a yawning hole in my soul that I had no idea how to piece back together.

This was my first experience losing someone close to me. I didn't know what this level of hurt felt like; I never grieved in that way before. Our connection was indescribable. From the moment when my eyes first laid eyes on him, I knew he was a special person. It was young love, but it was real love. You see, there's just a certain bond you have with the first love.

One weekend I was over at my other grandmother's house. All of the teenagers from that area would hang out and play outside games. That's when we first met. Our eyes locked, and he had the biggest smile on his face. I felt the connection before it was made official. We exchanged house numbers, and we were like Bonnie and Clyde, inseparable from there on out.

As we got older, we had on and off times, but we always had a level of respect for each other. He used to bring me roses and write me the sweetest poems. At such a young age, he knew how to be a gentleman. I remember we had a city festival called River Spree, and I needed some sneakers. I called and told him, and he rode to the mall on his bike to get them for me. We weren't old enough to drive yet, but he found ways to make sure he got to me. He was also a protector. If I were walking in the city from a relative's house back home, I would call him, and he would meet me so I wouldn't be walking alone. He was everything I could ever want and more.

Even though we were young, we had plans for a future together. We talked about getting a house and starting a family. I would make up children's names and send them to him. He was all for whatever I wanted. Not only were we a good match, but our families were close with each other. I soon learned my father used to date his aunt. His family loved me, and my family loved him. It was perfect. During the holidays, I would always stop by to visit his family. We still, to this day, call each other family. I refer to his cousins as my cousins, his aunts as my aunt. Our family bond was real.

When I moved to Greensboro, North Carolina, we were no longer in a relationship, but we remained friends. I would call him now and then to tell him about new opportunities, and one particular time, I called about my new boyfriend. He used to give me good advice, even

27

though he wasn't trying to hear that. Equally so, I didn't want to hear about his relationship either. Before I moved away, I was mad that he was talking to some girl, and I told my sister not to tell him that I was leaving. I wanted him to get mad at the fact that I was gone. He was talking to an older girl who had her own place. I was fresh out of school and living with my grandparents at the time. I felt like he was living the adult life faster than me. I couldn't wait to let him know when I had my own place.

One summer evening, I was in my new place, and there was a knock on my door. It was his uncle and my uncle's wife. They were related to each other some kind of way. She had just moved into my complex, and he had helped her move in. Again, our families were super close. His uncle was like, "I can't wait to tell him I saw you."

Well, fast forward to that winter. I was working at my second job at Target when I got called to the office for a phone call. This was a shock to me because I didn't know who would be calling my job. At the time, my sister was pregnant, so I thought maybe she had gone into labor. When I got to the phone, I found out my uncle's wife was on the other end.

"Hey, hold on for a second," she said.

Then, all of a sudden, I heard a voice say, "Yooooo!"

It was him. That's what he used to say when he called me. My heart skipped several beats. I was so excited!

"Where are you?" I asked him, and he replied that he was by my apartment.

He and his uncle had come together this time. I immediately told my supervisor that I had to leave and rushed to get there to see him. When I pulled up and saw his face, butterflies started fluttering in my stomach.

We embraced each other with the biggest hug. Afterwards, his uncle wanted a ride to the store. So, we took him there and back, then went to my apartment. I was so ready for him to see my new place, which I had laid out nicely. Since I'm a neat freak, I didn't have to scramble around to straighten up my place. Everything was tidy and smelled good. The aroma from a few wallflower plug-ins from Bath and Body Works filled the air.

Upon entering my townhome, he looked around with a big smile and jokingly asked, "Who lives here?"

I laughed and replied, "This is all mine."

While I gave him a tour of my apartment, he smiled all the way through. When we settled down to watch television, he noticed my coffee and end tables weren't sturdy. That's because I had put them together myself and didn't do a very good job. Being a true man, he asked for some tools and tightened up the table legs.

Still on a high because he was there with me at my apartment, I called my grandmother and said, "You're not going to believe who's sitting here in my living room."

When I told her who it was, she expressed her happiness for me. She could hear the excitement in my voice. So, of course, she shared in my joy.

He and I laughed, talked, and just enjoyed each other's company until we fell asleep. The next morning, my alarm clock awakened us. I had the alarm programmed so the radio would come on instead of it buzzing. At the set time, the radio began playing the song "My First Love" by Avant and Keke Wyatt. This song was so perfect and spoke volumes to us. As the music played, we listened to the lyrics and began talking about future plans. It's funny because we both still had plans of getting together and having our first child together.

Later that morning, we went to the mall to get a birthday gift for his niece, and after that, we said our goodbyes. That was the last time he came to Greensboro.

A few months later, while I was at work, he called. He said his father told him that he needed to get away from the city. So, he was thinking about moving to Greensboro to settle down. This was like music to my ears. I told him that sounded good and offered to help him get a job at UPS. I started envisioning how good everything would be with us together. However, months later, there wasn't any further talk about it. The year of his passing, he ended up having to get a cast on his leg due to an injury. I truly believe that is what kept him from moving right away.

In fact, I remember seeing him when I went back to my hometown one weekend to visit. He was riding with his cousin.

"Pack your stuff and come to Greensboro," I told him.

Looking at me, he replied, "I'm coming as soon as I get this cast off my leg."

Sad to say, he never made it.

One of the hardest days of my life was when I had to drive back home to say my final goodbye to him. As soon as I entered the city, there was a feeling of emptiness. The energy of the city was just off. I pulled up to my grandparent's house, walked in, and immediately burst out into tears.

"This can't be life. This can't be real! The love of my life is gone! He's gone!"

My grandfather knew how close he and I were, so much that my grandfather broke down in tears, too. This kind of hurt seemed unbearable.

A group of friends picked me up to drive me to the funeral home for the wake. As I prepared myself to view his body, all I kept thinking to myself was how would I go on. I walked into the room, and there he was—lying lifeless and cold.

As I stared at him, I kept saying, "Why didn't you come? You were supposed to come."

With tears streaming down my face and pain in my

heart, I didn't want to leave his side. As I stood over his body crying, I felt a tap on my left shoulder. I turned around abruptly, but there was no one there. I honestly felt like he had tapped me, letting me know he was still with me—right there by my side. Now it was up to me to find the strength to carry on, to keep pushing through the pain and excel, as he would have wanted.

As I sit here writing with tears in my eyes, I think about all of the lessons he taught me. One of the greatest was not settling. He showed me what true love was and how it was supposed to feel. Death is never easy, and one of the most difficult aspects of grief recovery is that grieving is a highly individualized process. This doesn't come with a how-to manual. The process is different for everyone, so it's impossible to know how much time it will take to heal, what the effects will have on you mentally, and what will trigger you to regress to an emotional and painful state. Even to this day, I have my triggers. It could be from his birthday to the day he transitioned to hearing that song play on the radio. I often play out in my mind how much different my life would be today if he were still here. And of course, there are times when you wish you could have done things differently to prevent such an outcome. We all may have those what-if moments.

Grief setbacks are very emotional, and recovery setbacks can happen at any time. Prime example, today, I felt normal and found myself experiencing an emotional breakdown as I relived our memories to write this chapter. It was very hard to do; I had to pull myself together and continue writing. There are good and bad ways to deal with grief setbacks. Bad ways of coping can consist of blaming yourself, blaming others, hiding your feelings, and shutting yourself away from everyone. All of these can have psychological effects on you, causing harm to your health. There were periods where I wished I could have drilled into him to change his environment. Even his sister looked at me one day and said she wished he would have left with me. I went through a period of shutting people out. I was hurt and felt emptiness. I didn't want to live without him. As time moved on, I found ways to pull myself together the best way I could. If you have ever experienced grief setbacks, you know firsthand this is a difficult process to overcome.

Here are a few good things to consider for dealing with grief recovery that I found online:

1. **Acknowledge the Experience.**
   Don't try to deny the fact that you are undergoing a painful experience. Resisting or hiding your pain will cause you further distress.

2. **Keep Busy.**

   Your emotions can be easily knocked off-balance when you're dealing with a grief setback. Get in the habit of sticking to your daily routines. Focus on eating, exercising, meditating, and doing activities that you enjoy. Also, try to keep yourself busy at work. Sometimes being idle can cause your mind to drift back into a grieving state.

3. **Spend Time with Supportive People.**

   Being around people with good energy can be very helpful. Whether it is family, a close friend, or a therapist, try to surround yourself with people who will listen to you and comfort you. This is subjective because I found peace being alone. Still, try to allow yourself to be around supportive people during difficult times. It can help prevent you from slipping into unhealthy habits.

4. **Focus on the Current Moment.**

   I read a book called *The Power of Now* by Eckhart Tolle, and within that book, it talked about how to handle the stresses of day-to-day life by living in the present moment. The author noted that every minute you spend worrying about the future or having regrets about the past is time wasted because all you have at this moment is the present—the now. All life is, is a series of present moments. Reliving past memories can trigger those original emotions. Truthfully, we're human, so we'll have these moments every now and then. But it's important not to stay in that space for too long. Try your best to focus on the present moment as long as you can.

5. **Seek Help.**

If, for some reason, you feel like you can't control your emotions or actions, it may be time to find a mental health professional to talk to. Look for free services offered online or in your community. Grief setback recovery is a process that requires strength, patience, support, and a lot of prayer. On your road to recovery, maintain a healthy mindset and engage in healthy activities.

Other Setbacks

Coping with life-changing setbacks can be difficult to navigate through. When it comes to these challenges, your attitude and approach determine whether you move forward or stay stagnant.

Throughout life, you will experience all sorts of setbacks. You may encounter setbacks such as death, troubled relationships, financial challenges, and so on. I'm sure you have endured one or more of these. Though you've dealt with these setbacks, you must not allow them to paralyze your progress in life. Whether you realize it or not, facing the obstacles has a way of making you stronger. Sometimes you have to dig deep to find your strength. There's a quote that comes to mind by Bob Marley that said, "You never know how strong you are until being strong is your only choice." Our personal strengths are part of what makes us unique. You must aim to get to the point where you can overcome anything life chooses to throw at you.

I have faced such phases of life wherein I felt that life was whipping my butt. Like, is this really life? But that never stopped me from finding a way to push through. All of the setbacks I faced made me more self-confident and self-sufficient. Of course, grief recovery was by far my toughest setback. Nothing else in life matters more to me than a life. My second setback was job losses that led to financial challenges. I went from making more than peers my age to being bogged down by a mountain of debt and having a depleted savings account. I'll discuss later how I overcame my financial challenges. These challenges taught me that it was okay to have a moment and go through the emotions. It also taught me how to pick myself up and allow my strengths to overshadow my weaknesses.

I had to figure out how to restart my life and try not to be in control of everything. I say this because, as soon as something happened that was beyond my control, I would sink to my lowest self. I felt powerless. There is only so much you can do, and the rest is up to the universal law or the powers that be. I have since learned not to worry so much about things beyond my control, understanding that life happens to us and for us. I look at life like this; everyone is given their own set of challenges in life to overcome. Yours and mine may be total opposites. However, this doesn't change the fact that we all have to deal with our experiences. Giving up is too easy, and in part, this is what separates the winners from the losers in life. It is essential to learn from life's experiences and disappointments so you can advance to the next level.

Overcoming your struggles is an up and down battle. The ups remind you of where you want to go, and the downs push you to get there. As with anything you want to achieve, you need to have a plan. Here is a simple guide:

Learn from the Experience – Embrace what happened and focus on regaining control of what you have control over.

Protect Yourself Against Extra Stress – Make sure you don't add any more negativity to your life. This is a great time to cut off anything and anyone that doesn't mean you well. Spend more time with positive people with good intentions.

Find Your Strength – One of the most effective ways to manage a setback is to deliberately think back to a major setback from your past. Think about how you were able to overcome that particular situation.

No one is exempt from the challenges of the world, and in today's world, social media has made it seem as if everyone is out here living their best lives problem-free. Most people will only show you the highlights of their lives while keeping their struggles and conflicts private. For this very reason, don't ever compare your life to anyone else's. Don't think life has singled you out to dump all its problems on. This isn't how this works. You can submit to being a depressed, negative-minded individual, or you can choose to overcome by being an inspirational, positive individual. How you adapt to challenges will determine your mindset, which your life depends on.

Chapter 4
Overcoming Self-Limiting Beliefs

Some of us have beliefs, which limit us in a lot of ways. These limiting beliefs impoverish our lives and prevent us from achieving our goals. Oftentimes, these self-limiting beliefs are adopted from childhood. Beliefs are nothing more than conditioned perceptions that are built upon over time from pain and pleasure. These memories are based on how we have interpreted and emotionalized our experience when attaching ourselves emotionally to people, things, and circumstances. We effectively build the foundation of our belief systems when beliefs are deeply ingrained into our nervous system due to repeated situations that prove their legitimacy. This will leave you feeling stuck in the present and become a hindrance to your future. To manifest your deepest desires, you have to challenge these limiting beliefs that hinder you from growth.

CHANGE IS TOO HARD

Let's face it, familiarity is safe and comfortable, and deep down, we prefer to play it safe than venture out into the unknown. Some people fear the unknown. When you're familiar with your current circumstance, it makes things more pleasurable. If you know for sure that you can survive a familiar problem, it might look like a better option than going down an unfamiliar path. We all crave some sense of certainty because it provides us with peace of mind and helps reduce stress, anxiety, and fear. If you already think change is too hard for you, you're pre-contemplating it. This may result from numerous failed attempts to change that have now stopped you from even trying.

Even though you may feel negative emotions, such as fear, regret, shame, or guilt, it is important not to stay stuck there. Having such negative emotions may trigger you to think about everything you're doing wrong or not doing. When taking a step to change, understand that it won't happen overnight. You will constantly have to work at it. Don't set goals that are too big; try to set small and measurable goals first. Over time, you will start to see cumulative change.

Do not allow yourself to get discouraged about what didn't happen or go as planned in the past. There were plenty of times that things for me went in the opposite direction. Even with these things happening, it didn't discourage me from wanting to try different things.

Don't resist change because of your fear of failing. Failure is a given and is part of the process. Get to a point where you see failure as a learning lesson in the process and not as an excuse to quit. It's never too late to hit the restart button or go back to finish something you gave up. Speaking from experience, there was a point when I wanted badly to get into real estate. I attempted to do so and failed at it. I knew it was a path that could lead to financial freedom; however, I couldn't connect the dots. So, what did I do? After not seeing results and not having a system, I gave up. I continued doing what was familiar. Even though I stayed in my comfort zone, I wasn't content. I had my hand in several things. I was a Jack-of-all-trades and the master of none. I'll go into details in a later chapter about how real estate came back full circle. What I want to stress to you is I didn't allow past failures to stop me from trying again.

I heard someone say there are two reasons why people think change is too hard:

1. We don't want it badly enough (lack of motivation)

   or

2. We don't know how to make it happen (techniques)

In my case, it was the fact that I didn't know what I was doing. I wanted it badly but maybe not as bad as I thought because if I did, I would have kept going until I saw results. In knowing what I know now, the only way I would not have been successful is if I quit. Looking back on this also made me realize I wasn't completely ready. Actually, that's one of the three reasons we don't welcome change: we're not ready, lack understanding, and want the result but not the process. Change has to take place first on a mental level and be accepted on an emotional level. We have to be okay with leaving our comfort zones and taking steps into the unknown.

As humans, we have an instinct to resist things that we cannot easily predict the outcome. One thing is for sure; change is uncertain, and we need to accept that. And the way we accept this truth is by facing our fears and giving ourselves permission to make mistakes. If you don't learn how to manage change, change will mismanage you. If you continue to think change is too hard, it will be. If you change your thinking, you can change your life. You can suffer the pain of change or suffer the pain of staying the same. It's a choice.

"There are no limits on what you can achieve with your life, except the limits you accept in your mind."

Brian Tracy

I DON'T HAVE THE RIGHT EDUCATION

In times such as these, we're living in an information age. Thanks to the internet, information is readily available at our fingertips. You know how much we have evolved if you are reading this and old enough to remember encyclopedias. It is so much easier to gain access to information nowadays.

Here's a little background on this remarkable evolution. The internet was developed during the 1970s by the Department of Defense and remained under government control until 1984. In the early 1990s, the World Wide Web was developed, in large part, for commercial purposes, and by the end of the 1990s, the world was fast becoming wired. That is so amazing to me. I say all of that to say this; one can obtain an education with a click of a button. Besides, Google and YouTube University have created a lot of Subject Matter Experts.

Don't allow the thought of not having the right education stop you from pursuing your goals. You have to choose whether or not you want to obtain the right education. And let me make one thing very clear. YOU DON'T HAVE TO BEAT YOURSELF UP IF YOU DIDN'T GO TO COLLEGE.

I had my own decision to make about attending college once I finished high school. It wasn't something forced upon me because of what my grandparents would have wanted for my life. Most parents force their children to go to college as if a college degree gives a person an automatic pass to be successful, which is far from the truth. During that stage in my life, college wasn't a part of my plan. I knew what I wanted to do after graduating from high school, and that was to hone in on my skill of being a cosmetologist. That's what I loved to do. So, for me, there was nothing I could see going to college for other than maybe a business class or studying to be a forensic pathologist. I was always intrigued by that and considered it until I saw they had to be on call to investigate crime scenes. Not that I didn't like the part about being at a crime scene. What I didn't like is that I wouldn't have control over my time. I digress. My main focus was to get a cosmetologist license so I could open my own salon one day. I was later able to execute the first part of my plan.

Having a skilled trade is just as good as having the right education. If you are good with your hands, be thankful and put your talents to use. We're living in such an age where people will frown upon certain careers that don't require a college education, or they consider you to be less than if you don't have a bunch of alphabets attached to your last name.

Let's take a plumber, for example. Someone may look down on a person who works in this field. But some plumbers are making more than those with a higher education. Experienced plumbers can make up to $200,000 a year. A *New York Times* article was posted that stated the following: "Even former Mayor Bloomberg of New York, a billionaire who knows a few things about making money, told listeners of his radio show that working as a plumber makes more financial sense for some students than attending an elite, four-year college." It then goes on to state, "Being a plumber, actually for the average person, probably would be a better deal, because you don't spend four years spending 40-50 thousand dollars tuition, and no income."

The Bureau of Labor Statistics states that plumbers and the related trades of pipefitters and steamfitters working in commercial and industrial settings earn well above the average median pay for all occupations. I found that article to be pretty interesting. Some people pursue a higher education but end up making less money than a plumber. Hell, some people even look down on cosmetologists. I considered getting a degree to prove a point. However, when I consulted a few successful people around me, they immediately told me that I didn't need to go to school. They geared me more to mentorships and certain books.

Social media has popularized degrees and HBCUs in our community. But what good is any of it if you're not fulfilled or up to your eyeballs in debt and can't find a job to offset your bills. Most people aren't even working post-graduation in their field of study. Let's talk about the statics about people chasing this so-called "right" education. In this study, we're talking about college grads. A recent report issued by Burning Glass finds that 43% of recent college graduates are underemployed. So, at the end of the day, you can have what is deemed the right education and still not be successful.

One of my favorite books, *Think and Grow Rich* by Napoleon Hill, had this to say in a section titled Insufficient Education: "This is a handicap which may be overcome with comparative ease. Experience has proven that the best–educated people are often those who are known as 'self-made' or self-educated. It takes more than a college degree to make one a person of education. Any person who is educated is one who has learned to get whatever he wants in life without violating the rights of others."

To further help you overcome this limiting belief, consider what *Think and Grow Rich* stated about two of America's successful men: "Thomas A. Edison had only three months of "schooling" during his entire life. He did not lack education, neither did he die poor. Henry Ford had less than a sixth grade "schooling" but he has managed to do pretty well by himself, financially." It then went on to say, "SPECIALIZED KNOWLEDGE is among the most plentiful, and the cheapest forms of service which may be had! If you doubt this, consult the payroll of any university."

Remember earlier in this chapter where I mentioned wanting to go to college to prove a point, but I was redirected to books and mentors? Well, I realized this all pointed to the acquiring of Specialized Knowledge. I started to acquire knowledge related to my specific business goals. I took up various business courses online tailored to my plans. I then learned how to organize and apply that knowledge. I also hired various mentors, which allowed me to shortcut my learning curve. I believe heavily in investing in myself in order to get to the level where I need to be. I didn't allow not having a degree or believing I didn't have the right education to stop me. Now I make more money than people I know who have degrees. I chose to acquire the right education according to what I wanted to accomplish.

I'm not saying for you not to go to college or get a degree. If you're passionate about something, see it all the way through. What I am saying is, don't just up and jump into school because it looks and sounds good or because that's what society pushes on you or the plan your parents have for you. You can easily be successful with Specialized Knowledge. Take me for example; I didn't need to learn algebra to be an investor. To this day, I haven't applied the general stuff taught to me in high school.

Overcome this belief by understanding what it is exactly that you want to do. What is it that you want to become? Get clear and laser-focused on your purpose, then start acquiring the proper knowledge to carry out your goals.

"Formal education will make you a living; self-education will make you a fortune."

Jim Rohn

I'LL NEVER BE SUCCESSFUL

Self-doubt is something we all experience. However, success cannot be achieved when you believe in thoughts that hold you back. I always felt deep down inside that I would be successful. I never believed it couldn't happen for me. However, I have been around individuals who possessed this type of mindset. I didn't come from a lineage of successful family members. There was no family blueprint;

I had to figure it out on my own. Someone once asked me if my mother and father were like me, and I told them no. To this day, I have accomplished more than both of them combined.

Growing up, if more were up for grabs, I always tried to obtain it. My mindset has always been if others can achieve success, so can I. Observing other people live certain lifestyles was evidence of what I could do. My thoughts shifted to how I could make success happen in my life. Who could I get to show me? You see, that's how my brain is wired. Instead of me thinking I would never be successful, I asked myself how I could be successful. It's all about your perspective. I first had to visualize what I wanted for my life and then figure out what I needed to do to get closer to making my vision a reality.

One thing about being successful is you determine what success looks like to you. Can you believe there are people you think are successful who don't feel they are successful themselves? It's true. This is primarily because they define their own success, and there will always be more levels they wish to reach. So, the question then becomes, at what point do you consider yourself successful? Is it when you reach a certain financial threshold? Is it when you have certain possessions or accolades? The list goes on and on.

For me, I consider myself successful in certain rooms I

enter and not as successful in other rooms—not in the sense that I haven't accomplished anything, but in terms of my level of accomplishments compared to that particular environment. In no way is that a bad thing. Being in a room where you're not the most successful or most intelligent person can cause you to level up. I'm sure you've heard the saying, "If you're the smartest person in the room, you're in the wrong room." So, if I feel like the underdog at that moment, it doesn't bother me one bit because I know I will soon be on their level.

There are people right now looking at your life and thinking you are successful because you have accomplished more than them. They could very well be looking at you as their next level. One thing I truly believe in is embracing and being appreciative of every level. Be grateful for all you've accomplished. I heard a quote one time that said, "Be thankful for your current position while plotting your next promotion." I couldn't have summed this up any better.

So, in overcoming this limiting belief, ask yourself what success looks like for you? Do you consider yourself successful now? Again, you determine what success looks like; therefore, no one can tell you what success should be.

Eliminate any self-doubt you have; turn that doubt into fuel for success. If you find yourself feeling stuck like you'll never be successful, work to identify where that way of thinking is coming from. Then use empathy to forgive yourself, or others, for creating that false belief inside of you in the first place. You have what it takes. Believe you can, and you're halfway there.

Chapter 5
Jealousy, Envy & Betrayal

As you start to understand that you're not a product of your environment, you will begin to navigate through your transitional phases, overcome your setbacks, and tackle your limiting beliefs. You'll soon encounter a new set of challenges. You are now evolving into a new being, and everyone isn't excited about your growth. There will be individuals who will discredit, devalue, or downplay your accomplishments. You'll even experience jealousy, envy, and betrayal on your journey to becoming successful. I know all too well.

It goes without saying that anything you do contrary to the "norm" will encounter resistance from other people. The sad truth is, this resistance can come from close friends and family. I've quickly learned that people who have an issue with your growth and success are deeply unhappy with those aspects of their lives.

FRIENDS

While writing this chapter, the song "What About Your Friends" by TLC popped into my head. The lyrics went like this: *What about your friends? Will they stand their ground? Will they let you down again? What about your friends? Are they going to be lowdown? Will they ever be around? Or will they turn their backs on you?*

Over the past few years, I've become increasingly successful with my life and business goals. I've worked hard to create a desired lifestyle. I have also been fortunate enough to connect with other successful individuals who were able to open up new doors and better opportunities for me. As I began to encounter such wins, I noticed certain behaviors with certain friends. I noticed that the people who I thought would be happy and supportive weren't at all. At some point, they started giving off a standoffish type of vibe. There's a quote that says, "Be the energy you want to attract." I tried to project the kind of energy I desired to get back, but I soon realized it wasn't reciprocated.

I'm the type of person who feels like I need to try to save

the world. I openly share knowledge and resources with anyone. Whatever I could do to help someone better themselves, I tried to assist. I especially wanted to do that for my friends. I enjoy seeing my people excel, and I am very supportive of their endeavors. Whenever my friends would get a new car, purchase a house, or open a business, I would get so excited for them. Not only did I share in their excitement, but I wanted them to share all the details. Others' success stories are motivation to me.

On the flip side of this, I noticed the feeling wasn't mutual with certain friends. This was hard to grasp at first. I remember the time when I purchased my car. I was so happy and couldn't wait to tell a few people. Well, one person seemed to be more concerned about *how* I got approved for the loan than being happy about me getting it. And when it came to my house and businesses, it was no different. It was like they didn't want to hear about it; no congratulatory responses or anything. One day, I overheard a conversation while calling someone to tell them about one of my recent accomplishments. As the person answered the phone, I heard them tell someone in the background, "Oh, this is Andrel. She's calling to brag again." I guess they didn't realize the phone had already picked up. I was shocked! I couldn't believe that's how they felt. I didn't say anything at the time, but I did commit her comment to memory.

Anything I accomplished and told them about, they viewed it as me being braggadocious. As the years passed, I watched how things became more like a competition. If I presented them with some type of opportunity, they wouldn't want anything to do with it because they didn't come up with the idea first. They wanted to be in charge. Regardless of how people viewed or treated me, I still tried to remain supportive and cordial. Sometimes, I constantly battle between treating others how they treat me and treating them how I want to be treated. The humanitarian in me is always trying to help. But, at some point, I realized I had to stop expecting me from other people. Their morals and ethics weren't the same. A person's actions will tell you everything you need to know.

Knowing how some friends viewed me, I refrained from saying too much. I started withholding certain information from certain people that I so badly wanted to share. You might expect jealousy from other people, but it impacts you differently when it comes from people you call your friends. I've never really understood how someone could be envious of someone else's accomplishments.

FAMILY

Blood makes you related; love and respect make us family. Sometimes we feel a moral obligation to get along with family. Sadly, not all members will bond. To create a strong bond, family must respect differences.

Back in 2008, I had a housewarming party. As guests would arrive, they took their shoes off at the door upon entering my home. It wasn't something required; they took the initiative on their own. However, I respected their decision to do so. I remember standing at the door watching my mother and aunt pull up in the driveway. My mother came in the door, and my aunt followed. Once my aunt entered, she immediately noticed everyone's shoes in the foyer.

My aunt turned around, and with her nose in the air, she stated, "Oh, I'm not going in there because I have to take my shoes off."

I explained to her that she didn't have to and that everyone else did by choice.

She proceeded to say, "That's okay. I'll wait in the car." Then she turned around and walked out.

Remember, just because someone is family doesn't mean they won't be jealous of you. This particular aunt was always negative, and she always had an underlying issue with me. For one, she thinks I act bougie. She has said slick comments to me before, but still, I respected her. After a while, you learn to become immune to a person's words and actions towards you. Nothing she says at this point surprises me. My success and growth irk the hell out of her.

She has even gone as far as to remove me from her Facebook page. I've never done anything to this lady. She is obviously fighting some internal issues.

At this stage in my life, I have a low tolerance for foolishness. Now when we meet at family functions, I don't even bother going out of my way to speak to my aunt as I would typically do. It's clear she doesn't care for me, and I'm not going to fake it as though everything is cool between us. If family doesn't act like family, it may just be time to cut them off.

OUTSIDERS

We tend to avoid severing ties with our family members; we can often do this with friends. Society has pushed a false narrative that tells us that our family is an unbreakable bond. However, it is reasonable to cut all ties if they are negative and toxic. Set boundaries and be assertive when enforcing them.

When you're a threat, you become a target. Social media has heightened the level of jealousy one may experience. I found this out quite early.

I was in a relationship, or somewhat of a relationship, which sparked a jealous female to take things overboard. Never in my life have I experienced such hate and jealousy.

It all happened around the height of my accomplishments.

Around 2006, I met a gentleman, and we ended up in a relationship after about a year. I really didn't approve of his lifestyle during this time and tried to push him to do other things. I could see the potential there and wanted to help him evolve. When things didn't change, he and I became distant but were still involved. As a woman, we can pick up on things that aren't right. They call it women's intuition. Well, during our little off times, I felt he was involved with someone else. I recall asking this to be made clear to me through prayer. And guess what? It was soon revealed.

One Sunday, while sitting in church, I remember the pastor saying, "You keep asking God why things are going so crazy. God is about to put something in front to show you."

Well, I was at work on a Friday, and one of my coworkers mentioned she wanted to hang out later that evening. Since it was the weekend, I was cool with going. We both decided we were going to the mall to find something to wear, but we wanted to go at different times. She wanted to go directly after work, and I wanted to take a nap first before going. For some reason, I was adamant about the time. We then both agreed to meet at seven o'clock p.m.

On my way to the mall, one of my other friends

happened to call to see what I was doing. Once I told her that I was going to the mall, she suggested I check out a new store that had just opened. So, I decided to make that store my first stop upon arriving. As I entered the new store, I quickly scanned the aisles. Not seeing anything I liked, I walked out. As soon as I left the store, another friend called and asked me where I was, and I informed her that I had just walked out of this particular store in the mall. She said that she was in the mall, too, and told me to go back into that store because she was on her way there.

After entering the store for a second time, I took my time perusing through the racks while waiting on her. A few short minutes later, I lifted my head from looking at a shirt and noticed my guy friend speaking with a female in the store. In my mind, I was thinking he saw me come into the store and stopped in. He had a lot of female friends, so I didn't think too much of it. Well, after realizing he hadn't seen me, I decided to walk over to them. As soon as he saw me, his face lit up as if he had seen a ghost. While observing his actions, I knew this female wasn't just a friend.

I remember him saying, "Oh, hey. You're in here trying to find something for tonight?"

After I answered him, I asked him a question of my own. "Are you going to introduce me to your friend?"

He did but only addressed us by our names, no titles. He then started sweating profusely, and she quickly wiped the sweat from his forehead like it was natural for her to do. Once she did that, I knew there was something more between them. So, I began to question her, asking how she knew him. When she stated he was her boyfriend, he didn't say one word. I told her that I thought that was funny because he and I were in a relationship, too.

She then stated, "I don't see how that's possible because we live together."

A bit naïve, I thought to myself, *Why would she say it's impossible when I know the truth?*

At that moment, I thought back to the message I had received in church. God was showing me why things were going so crazy. Needless to say, that evening didn't go as planned. I canceled my plans to go out in order to process all of what happened. Shortly after the ordeal, the guy called me to say it wasn't what I thought and that he knew her for years before meeting me but didn't know how to tell her. After he and I spoke that night, I changed my phone number. I didn't want to hear anything else. Well, this situation ended up creating a very jealous female.

A few months later, while at work, I noticed a new training class walking in the hallway, and in that line was the female from the encounter. I had to do a double-take.

God, what is the lesson in this? I said to myself. *Why is she at my job?*

The answers to those questions were soon revealed, as

well. One evening not too long after she started the job, my guy friend came to my apartment. As soon as I opened the door, he asked me about changing my number. I told him that I didn't have anything else to say and had seen all that I needed to see. Can you believe he was still trying to plead his case? When he looked around the apartment and noticed all of my things packed up in boxes, he asked where I was moving. I told him that I would be moving in with my aunt and quickly changed the subject. During this time, I had started the process of building my first home, but I kept it a secret from him because I didn't want him to know where I lived.

As we were sitting there, I asked him was he aware that the female was working at my job. That's when he told me that she and her best friend stalked my social media page and found out I worked there. He added that she was being funny by applying and ended up getting hired. The series of events that followed were crazy. I was approaching a major milestone—preparing to close on my first home. As the saying goes, "New level, new devil." I literally felt that way. As soon as I started focusing on my goals, there came a distraction.

I have never understood why a woman would be jealous of other women, and in my case, especially over a man. Maybe it's because they feel like their position is threatened. I've never experienced this level of jealousy in my life. Once this female found out I had built a home, she looked up my property information and drove by. She then posted pictures of a slightly bigger home than mine with captions about her property value, even pointing out her huge backyard. I guess she wanted to post something she thought was better than mine. The thing about that was she didn't own the home; she was renting it.

He later came back to tell me all of these things. He said she was on it once she found out I had a house. He even confirmed that's how he found my address because she drove him around my subdivision, asking him if he knew anyone who lived there. This took the jealously to a whole new level for me. Everything I set out to do, she also did. She even began dressing like me. And, of course, when you have a lot of good things going for you, some people will try to bring you down by pointing out your flaws. Fake pages were created on social media to attack anything I was accomplishing. However, I have always been ambitious. So, the more they attacked, the more I set out to accomplish.

An old pastor once said, "A car needs both positive and negative energy in order to run." While I appreciated the positive people in my life, I now had to learn how to push past the negativity I faced. The thing about this is, my experience with the young lady lasted for several years. She disliked me and all that I had set out to accomplish. It was almost like she had something to prove, whereas the only person I had to prove anything to was myself. In the end, what she thought would tear me down helped to propel me.

In certain moments of our lives, we may not understand why things are happening. Then when we later look back on it, we can see the lesson. I realized all of what I experienced helped me. Instead of retaliating, I focused my energy on my goals and business ventures. I'm good at turning negative situations into positive situations. As you encounter jealousy from outsiders, remember that it is a direct reflection of who they are. They may be intimidated by your success. Keep thriving anyway. They will eventually fade away.

I think anyone who has accomplished great things will experience some type of jealousy from outsiders. I have witnessed this too often on social media. Think about it, have you ever seen negative comments under someone's post? There are people whom we now call "internet trolls" who find pleasure in spewing negative remarks. These individuals will always have something to say and attack with criticism. Some people call them haters; however, jealousy can ferment into hate. Hate has different phases. When these people attack you, they are imposing their self-hate onto you.

Outsiders who are indirectly jealous of you can also be dream killers. As you're growing, be mindful of who you're sharing your dreams with. I worked in a salon for a few years, and I could pick up on the individuals who didn't care for my growth. I would mention how I was working on a few projects, and they would always have something negative to say. I reached a point where I would only discuss certain things with certain coworkers and a few clients who I trusted. I found that the coworkers who gravitated towards me were interested in bettering themselves. They took things I would share as valuable takeaways.

One Saturday afternoon, it was somewhat slow. So, a few stylists got together to talk about finances. I shared with them some information they could implement to improve their financial situations. Suddenly, here comes the salon owner, who wasn't too fond of the stylists huddling together to talk. She especially didn't like it if I was in the mix. She immediately broke up our huddle by telling us that we needed to start cleaning the salon.

The owner was the kind of person who didn't want to listen to anyone's ideas on how she could grow; it's like she was okay with being stagnant in her life. In addition, she was the type who thought she was always right. So, of course, she felt some type of way when we all came together to talk about changing for the better. She would inflict her negative attitude on others; this was reflected in the high turnover rate. It was so bad that sometimes you could walk in and feel the tension in the air. Needless to say, she couldn't keep good stylists around for long. My reason for staying was to reach a certain goal. However, I quickly realized it wasn't the environment I needed to be in.

Despite the negativity, I left on good terms when I decided to part ways from the establishment. I even typed up a professional letter thanking her for the opportunity to work there. Most stylists would just quit and not think twice about giving any notice.

Working in an atmosphere with dream killers taught me that everyone isn't meant to see your vision. Your vision was given to you for a reason. I also learned you can't share your ideas with everyone. In a lot of cases, you'll want to keep your mouth closed until you have completed what you set out to do.

Think back to a time when you told someone about something you wanted to do. They may have talked against it or gave you their version of how it should be. It's okay to get feedback. What's not okay is for someone to try to kill your dream or make you feel like you are not equipped enough to carry it through. They may tell you that your goals are unrealistic, unsustainable, too risky, farfetched, and on and on. Steve Harvey once said, "If you want to kill a big dream, tell it to a small-minded person." You see, beneath the sarcasm, criticism, and tough exterior that dream killers project, they feel afraid deep down. They're worried you might actually make something great of your life. You accomplishing your dreams might make their excuses for why they've given up and settled less valid.

Guard your dreams at all costs. Some people will try to stop you from taking action because actions defy their way of life. You dominating your goals and dreams will breed jealousy. Evaluate your surroundings and take notice if you have any of these types of people around you. It's perfectly fine to start eliminating these people from your life and surround yourself with people who believe in you and what you're trying to accomplish. Listen to your intuition and pursue your dreams with confidence. Believe in yourself and make the impossible possible without giving thought to how someone may feel about your accomplishments. Don't allow people with negative outlooks to deter you from your journey.

"Keep away from people who try to belittle your ambitions. Small people always do that, but the really great make you feel that you, too, can become great."

Mark Twain

FRENEMIES

LAW 2: NEVER PUT TOO MUCH TRUST IN FRIENDS, LEARN HOW TO USE ENEMIES. FRIENDS WILL BETRAY YOU. HIRE FORMER ENEMIES; THEY'LL BE LOYAL"

– THE 48 LAWS OF POWER

They say keep your friends close and enemies closer. But what do you do when they're one and the same? I think most of us have had at least one or two frenemies. The good news is any relationship that doesn't make us feel good or contribute to our well-being doesn't have to be tolerated. Sure, we may care for these people, but when they don't genuinely care for you, exercise your right to limit the relationship or eradicate them all together. Doing so can be empowering and wonderful.

I recall disconnecting with a friend I had known for several decades. Even though it was hard to do at the time, her actions never changed. So, dissolving the friendship was the best thing to do. Grab some wine, sit back, and read about how this journey began and ended.

When I first moved to Greensboro, I was excited about experiencing new opportunities and meeting new people. This was a fresh start for me, and I was super excited. It was something about moving from a small town to a bigger city that I wanted to embrace. I met my first set of friends through my job at the UPS call center. Just like a kid in a new school, I walked around observing people, trying to determine who might be cool to hang out with. I quickly connected with girls from my training class and met a few others who weren't in the class.

One evening, while in the cafeteria, I met this girl who seemed pretty cool. We would speak often. I'm not sure how our initial conversation started, but I remember her telling me that she, too, had just moved to Greensboro from a smaller town. So, because we had that in common, we exchanged numbers and began meeting up after work. Everything seemed to be going well with our friendship. We shared plenty of laughs and would occasionally take road trips. I even met my first boyfriend through her. This was interesting.

One weekend, she asked if we could get together so I could do her hair, and I agreed. She came over to my apartment for a quick hairstyle, which I did without charging her. I didn't think too much of it because she had brought some steaks over for us to cook. I figured it was our unspoken barter. That night, she spoke on the phone with her guy friend, who wanted to bring his son over for her to watch for a little while. She asked if it was okay, and I didn't see a problem with that. So, her guy friend came over, and we were introduced to each other. He dropped his son off and left. When he called a couple of hours later to let her know he was on his way back, he asked if it would be okay if his cousin came with him. I told him that was fine. Well, long story short, his cousin ended up being my boyfriend.

So now, we had something else in common. Our boyfriends were cousins. This was pretty cool because the four of us would spend a lot of time together and go on double dates.

Even though she and I had hit it off as friends, there were other girls with who I also became close. They were from High Point, North Carolina, a neighboring city to Greensboro. I'll just refer to them as the locals. The locals and I would also meet up after work and even took trips out of town. Making new friends was a breeze for me. I was settling in nicely.

Well, because we all worked together, it was only a matter of time before my friends would connect with each other. I introduced everyone and assumed we were all friends at this point. One day, we were all talking about a party that was coming up. The locals invited me, and because they knew the other girl through me, she also received an invitation. I'll just refer to her as the ex-friend from here on out. We all met at the local event and had a great time. Everyone was getting along well. The ex-friend was more my friend than theirs, but we were all cordial...or so I thought.

As time went by, I noticed certain behaviors with the ex-friend that I didn't agree with. This was the first of many signs that revealed her true character. One night, the locals and I were invited over to her home before we went out that night. We were all dressed and just waiting for her to get ready. We sat around talking, laughing, and having a few drinks in the meantime.

A few minutes into our girl talk, she told us to come into her bedroom because she wanted to show us something. What she showed us tickled us all. We were just having good ol' girl fun. As the locals were leaving out of the room, I followed behind. That's when her house phone began ringing. Back then, people still had house phones and Caller ID. Well, being that I was the last to leave out, I glanced at the Caller ID and saw the name and number of my local friend's boyfriend. At that moment, I was confused. Why would my local friend's boyfriend be calling my ex-friend? For the sake of not killing the vibe, I didn't speak of it to either of them that evening. Oh, I forgot to mention that my local friend's boyfriend also worked with us. Everyone knew they were together because they always hung out at work. So, my ex-friend very much knew that my local friend was in a relationship with the guy.

At that moment, I started looking at her differently. She

came off as being sneaky. Entertaining your friend's boyfriend is against the girl code. Men will be men regardless, but there are certain things women shouldn't do, especially if you're in the same circle. Men come and go, but your true girlfriends will always be around.

Eventually, I told my local friend what I noticed that night so she could be aware of what was going on. Soon after that, the locals fell back from dealing with my ex-friend, and so did I to a certain extent. But it wasn't long before I had my own encounter with her. I surely didn't think she would cross me. After all, we were closer than her and the locals.

As years went by, I switched jobs, but my ex-friend and I still kept in contact. We didn't talk every day, but we would meet up now and then. During this particular time, I had two jobs, one of which was at a cell phone kiosk at the mall. One week while I was at work, a guy approached the kiosk to pay his cell phone bill. He then asked for my name and number. I gave him my name but declined to give him my number, so he gave me his.

One of my coworkers, who knew who he was, said to me, "Girl, you don't know who that is?" All I remember responding was that he was cute and looked like trouble. We both laughed. She then advised me that he was the first cousin of a rap artist named Jim Jones. I simply replied, "Okay." I have never been the star-struck type, putting celebrities on a pedestal. Needless to say, I still didn't call him.

A couple of weeks later, the same guy approached me while I was at work, asking me why I hadn't called him yet and being very adamant about wanting me to call. Again, he gave me his number and then walked away, going inside a store adjacent to the kiosk. The next thing I knew, I looked up and noticed he was walking back towards me with the sales associate from that store. Holding a dress on a hanger, he had come to ask me if I liked it. I was in a state of shock. I looked at both him and the sales associate as if to say, *Did this guy really just come out of the store with this dress?* It was hilarious, but I loved his effort. After telling him that I liked the dress, he purchased it and gave it to me. At this point, I decided to give him a call.

One afternoon, he called and asked if I would like to meet him after work since he was in town for a few days. I agreed to it. There was a restaurant near the mall where he wanted to meet. When I arrived, I was the only female there; he was there with a few guy friends. So, I decided to call my ex-friend to see if she could join me. She stated she had her son with her, but she agreed to come. This later turned out to be a bad idea.

When she arrived, I introduced her to everyone. During our conversation at the table, I mentioned to her that he was the first cousin of Jim Jones; they actually resembled each other a lot. We all sat around talking and enjoying the atmosphere until it was time to leave. My guy friend started talking to her son about some video game and told him that he could pick him up one day so they could play together with his daughter, who was close to my ex-friend's son's age. One thing about this guy, he loved kids. I was standing there when he gave his number to her, so it wasn't anything he was trying to hide. All he knew was my ex-friend was my homegirl.

That night, I followed her back to her house to hang out for a few. When I shared with her about how I had met him and the dress ordeal, she looked at me and said, "Girl, you hit the jackpot!"

I will never forget that. She obviously saw an opportunity, and this was later confirmed.

One weekend, my guy friend was back in town and asked me if I wanted to hang out. Since I was free that weekend, we decided to meet up. I looked forward to seeing him because he treated me like a queen every time we were together. When he called, I was at my ex-friend's house. So, I figured I would have him pick me up and leave my car there.

We talked while riding around and even stopped by to visit a few of his relatives because he wanted to introduce me to everyone, which I thought was very nice of him. We enjoyed each other's company until it started getting late. I asked him to take me to get my car, and on the way back, he said I could follow him to a restaurant so we could grab something to eat. Once I returned to my car, I didn't bother calling my ex-friend or knocking on her door because it was getting late. I just hopped in my car and proceeded to follow him. After dinner, we sat in his car in the parking lot; it had to be close to midnight by then. As we were talking, his phone began to ring, and he extended it to me.

"It's your girl," he told me.

When I said hello, I could hear her stutter slightly as if she was shocked I had answered.

"Hey," she finally said. "I was just making sure you picked your car up."

I told her yes and ended the call. Two things about her call made me raise an eyebrow. One, she could have known the answer to her question by simply looking out her window, and two, why was she calling his phone and not mine? If I had to guess, she probably didn't expect me to still be with him, and if I weren't present, there is no telling what she would've said to him. Immediately, I thought back to the incident involving her, my local friend, and my local friend's boyfriend. At that moment, I lost complete trust in her.

After that incident, I began distancing myself from her. Ironically, I ran into a mutual friend of ours in a local store, and to make small talk, I asked if she had spoken to the ex-friend.

"Girl, no," she replied. "I stopped talking to her when I told her that my boyfriend and I were going to stop by her house, and she answered the door wearing lingerie."

This opened up a whole conversation right there in the aisle. I shared with her the incident that had happened involving my guy friend. That's when the mutual friend told me that she knew of the guy through my ex-friend because of homecoming one year. My ex-friend had called her to tell her that Jim Jones, another rapper, and my guy friend would be at a hotel room after the concert, and she invited her to come. So, it was apparent my ex-friend was in contact with this guy without mentioning anything about it to me. After hearing this, I wrote her off in my book. As far as the guy and me, we were still good friends, but I was back with my ex at the time. Besides, he was always on the go, so it wasn't anything I could see being long-term.

This situation numbed me because I couldn't understand why someone who called you their friend would do something like that. I mean, I thought we were cool, but there was clearly an underlying issue with her.

About six or seven years later, we reconnected on Facebook. Around this time, I was sharing my journey about finances and putting content together to help others. I noticed my ex-friend would engage with my post and share my content with her friends. Up until this point, I hadn't conversed with her about why I stopped talking to her. I put it behind me and moved on.

During this time, my personal brand was taking off. I had taken several certification courses and hired a few coaches to help me take things up a notch. My followers started to grow, and I began getting requests for me to speak at various events. Things in my life were shifting in an upward direction. While witnessing my success, the ex-friend reached out on multiple occasions to invite me to gatherings. One year, I recall she asked if I could make her birthday dinner, but I couldn't. She sent me a message on Facebook soon after stating we needed to catch up. I had a prior engagement to attend, so again, I had to decline.

Always busy attending some event or seminar, it was hard for me to find the time for us to catch up. Not to mention, I was also working multiple jobs. Speaking of which—one day, while working at the salon, I had the privilege of meeting a local beauty icon named Joe Dudley. Joe Dudley, who believed in entrepreneurship, extended a personal invitation for me to attend his mastermind meetings at his house. I'll speak more about this encounter in a later chapter.

Being the humanitarian that I am, I'm always trying to share knowledge and connect people in order to help them. So, one day, I sent a message on Facebook to my ex-friend and another friend, inviting them to the meeting. It would give them a chance to rub shoulders with a local millionaire, receive his wisdom, and network with others.

When I extended the invite to my ex-friend, she was elated. She told me that she didn't have many business-minded friends and needed to surround herself with more of those types of people. Of course, I was happy I could make that happen for her.

On the day of the meeting, I sent another message via Facebook to advise her of the time I was leaving. We agreed to meet up at a local gas station and follow behind each other. Once we arrived and entered Mr. Dudley's home, I introduced her to everyone and proceeded with the meeting agenda. After the event, my ex-friend expressed how much she needed to be in that atmosphere and thanked me again for inviting her. Overall, the meeting went well. Even though I had my reservations about her, I was willing to past that and give things another try.

Mr. Dudley had the meetings faithfully every week. While I didn't attend all of them, I stopped by every once in a while. I recall one specific time when I went straight to the meeting fresh off the highway from DC after having missed a few weeks. That particular evening when I walked in, I noticed my ex-friend was there. We hadn't talked about her going, but that wasn't a problem with me. However, she was walking around with the lead organizer, who was a male, and handing out papers. Come to find out, she was now a board member for a recent project, and I knew nothing of this until that night. I had mixed emotions at this point. I was excited to see her take off, but at the same time, I was curious why she didn't tell me that she was going to or had joined a new board.

We spoke briefly after the meeting about my trip to DC. During our conversation, she kept saying we needed to catch up. I told her that I had gone to a business workshop and was scheduled to fly out to Dallas that following weekend to meet my mentor, but we would connect.

Fast forward, after I came back from Dallas, she sent me a message to do dinner. I didn't have anything planned, so I agreed. We met up that day at a local restaurant around 3:00 p.m. As soon as the waiter finished taking our order, my ex-friend took out a notepad and pen and started asking me business questions. I didn't think much of it at the time, but she got a lot of branding tips and a full lecture out of me for free. Then she started updating her social media platforms right there at the table. The things I told her were the same things I was training my mentees how to do. But this was a "friend," right?

We didn't leave the restaurant until 7:00 p.m. Now granted, our conversation wasn't all about business, but we spent 95% of the time with her picking my brain. She could have at least offered to pay the tab in exchange for the amount of information she received, especially knowing that was her intention anyway. After all, I had just spent over three thousand dollars on a mentor to help me. If I could invest in myself, she certainly could have compensated me for the information I gave her.

Later, I discussed this with a friend, who told me that my ex-friend was using me. Our conversation prompted me to post a question on Facebook. The question was: *Should friends and family expect services for free or a discount?* I had an upcoming class that I was teaching about creating digital products for passive income, which my ex-friend kept asking about prior. Ironically, after I made that post, she told me that she would pay for the class.

At this point, I started to observe her more closely because when you're successful in certain areas, people will want to cling to you for their own personal gain and wrongful intentions. It was only a matter of time before her hand was revealed.

Every year for Mr. Dudley's birthday, he would have an event that would include a panel of speakers and then throw a black-tie gala the next day. I had invited my ex-friend to the celebration the first year we started back talking, but the following year, things were different between us. Since I hadn't received one phone call or text from her to ask if I was going, I decided not to call or text her either. I had made plans to attend the speaking panel but not the gala scheduled for the following night.

On the day of the event, I entered the lobby area and was greeted by several individuals from the weekly meetups. We talked briefly, and then I continued to make my way towards the vendors. Upon entering that area, I saw her off to the side wearing an event badge. She came over to me with a shocked look on her face.

"I didn't know you were coming," she said.

"I always come to these events," I replied.

She appeared as though she didn't want me in the mix.

I was starting to question her motives since, to me, it seemed like she was after success by any means necessary, even if it meant stepping on someone else's toes.

It was now time for the panel of speakers, so I made my way into the ballroom, found a seat, and sat down to listen to the first presenter. I sat towards the back of the room to be closer to an outlet to charge my phone. She entered and sat a few seats over on the row where I was sitting. As the first presenter started speaking, I quickly realized he was the guy in a documentary about black wealth. I recalled reaching out to him years before to ask him about one of his investing strategies. I had no idea he was going to be a presenter. I thought to myself, *This is the Law of Attraction.* He gave a powerful speech, even mentioning some cool things about a trip to Cairo, Egypt, but said nothing about that particular strategy.

After he finished, I decided to meet him in the vendor's

area to inquire. As I approached his table, another young lady was speaking with him. So, I respectfully waited until they were done. Once the young lady walked off, he greeted me, and I told him that I had watched his documentary and wanted to know if he still did those types of investment strategies. When he replied that he did, I began to tell him that I was in finances, as well. As we were talking, the ex-friend walked over, stood directly in front of me, and introduced herself while shaking his hand. I immediately stepped back, in awe at how she interrupted us.

When he turned his attention back to me, he expressed that he wanted to connect further and go out for dinner. He also advised me that he was doing free training the next day, which was happening right before the gala, and asked for my email. The ex-friend barely spoke to me after the event, only briefly about the training the next day.

The next day arrived, and there was an email about the class start time. I made my way to the training, but there was a mix-up when I arrived at the hotel. They didn't have the correct room where the class was being held. I saw two other females standing in the hall looking confused, as well. They, too, were looking for the training room. At that point, I continued to walk around, hoping to see someone. I ran back into the same two ladies, but they weren't having any luck locating the room either. I decided to call the ex-friend to see if she had any other details. Her phone rang several times before going to voicemail. A few seconds later, I ran into her turning a corner. Her phone was visible in her hand, but she didn't answer my call for some reason. When I asked her where the training class was being held, she looked at me with a straight face, stated the name of the room, and then added, "It said that in the email." Her tone and facial expression indicated that she was not too excited to see me there. It ended up being a room change at the last minute, and a few of us didn't get the email notifying us of the change.

When the training began, the speaker started talking about investing strategies. He mentioned we could partner with his company and take his class being held in another state the following month. Interested in learning more, I had already planned to go. Training went on for about an hour before the ex-friend decided to get up and leave out. I figured she had to get ready for the gala; I wasn't going to that. Even though she was sitting in the row behind me, she didn't bother saying bye or anything. She just up and left. Because of our history, I knew her intentions were to throw herself at him during the gala. Sure enough, his assistant told me about a month later that's what happened.

We didn't communicate again until about two days later when I made a post on Facebook saying I wanted to go to Cairo. I heard so many good things about it at the event that I put it out there to my friends. Underneath my post, she commented, *Funny you should mention that. I'm going.* In response to her comment, I asked, *When and with who?* But there were crickets. You'll soon find out why.

When I contacted her on Facebook about the upcoming training, she told me that she planned to attend. We even talked about going half on the investment. I had a few questions for him, and I told her that I would reach out to him about it. She proceeded to tell me to give her my questions, and she would ask him for me when she spoke with him. I thought that was hilarious. Clearly, she didn't want the man to talk to me.

She told me, "If he makes me some money, he can be boo or bae. I'm going to take one for the team with him."

What struck me the wrong way was when she told me to "take one for the team" with another successful guy who I told her about. The other guy and I weren't a good fit at all, but she was trying to push me off on him.

"It'll all pay off later when we're paid!" she had said. "Pick his brain, and I'll handle this end. Deal? The deal is just between us."

With her motives becoming clear, I told her no and that I wasn't interested in the other guy.

She replied by saying, "Does looks even matter these days? I keep asking myself. A lot of these guys ain't cute, but they're smart as hell. And I love a smart man."

We had both been around each other long enough to know the types of men we would entertain. The presenter was more my type than hers, but I didn't pursue him. The way I operate, if a friend of mine shows interest in someone, I let my friend have at it. If a guy is interested in a friend, I let him have at it. I don't insert myself to stop anything. She saw an opportunity to come up; she saw money and didn't want me in the way of that.

As the days went by, my ex-friend and I started discussing plans to attend the out-of-state training. We wanted to go half on the investment because it would be our first time doing a strategy like this, and we didn't want to put too much into it starting off. I decided to put the past behind me and focus my mind on the new venture.

Training day arrived. I met her at her house, and we rode together in the same car. During the road trip, we started reminiscing about the good times of our friendship. Even then, I didn't mention why I had stopped speaking with her the first time; I wanted to keep things cordial. However, when we arrived at the training office, her whole demeanor changed.

The things I witnessed that weekend were unreal. So much so that I wished I had a camera rolling. She was going in for the kill. I remember in one instance, she bent over near him to charge her phone. I mean, she didn't squat like a lady; she bent all the way over to catch his eye. He turned and looked at her, then glanced over his assistant and smirked. I was there to learn about getting my investments going, but she had her own motive. Every time he approached me, she would come over, wanting to be right there in the mix. It started to be unmistakably obvious. I noticed the other attendees watching the ex-friend with a side-eye.

After training, everyone was invited out to dinner. Since there were about fifteen of us, the wait to get into the establishment was rather long. If it hadn't already been proven before, what happened at this dinner showed me that she didn't want me in the way.

Several of the people from our group had gone into the restaurant while the others waited outside. As I walked in with his assistant, she pointed out the ex-friend's behavior and then told me about how she was acting at the gala. After about ten minutes, I decided to walk back outside to where I had left the ex-friend. As soon as I stepped out the door, I noticed she was standing off to the side conversing with him. Wanting to show her how it feels to be interrupted, I walked right up to them.

"Don't forget to send me that paper," she told him.

"What paper?" I quickly chimed in.

"Oh, nothing," she replied softly. "Just something that he and I talked about."

The trainer looked at me and said, "Cairo."

I promise, when he told me that, she turned her head so fast to look at me that it was almost like a scene in *The Exorcist*. She looked like she had just seen a ghost! Remember when I mentioned earlier about my Facebook post and how she commented that she was going but did not divulge when or with whom? Well, this is why.

I turned and looked at her while replying to him, "That's funny; I posted on Facebook that I wanted to go to Cairo."

She was silent!

"Oh, you can come," he told me. "My team is going back there to shoot a film, but anyone can go. Here's the travel agent's number that's handling everything,"

At that moment, I realized she and I couldn't continue being friends. After that, the energy between us was off, and I knew I couldn't trust her if she tried to keep something like that from me. Unless it was about the investment, I didn't have too much to say to her.

The next day, we met back up with the trainer to go over the details, but the ex-friend backed out, no longer wanting to split the investment cost with me because she claimed she was looking for more profit margin. Because I had come all that way, I approached the trainer to see if another person from the class wanted to go half with investing. He stated we could wait until the following month and invest in a different state, and I was okay with that.

As he and I were walking, he looked at me and said, "I've been trying to talk to you all weekend. I wanted to ask to take you out, but someone keeps blocking me."

I laughed because all of her attempts at trying to throw herself at him didn't work. The whole time, he had his eye on me. Not only that, but I'm sure he recognized her actions but didn't care. A guy like him was used to women going after him for the wrong reasons. Me, on the other hand, was strictly about business. I guess he recognized that, too.

Later that night, he had to stop and speak at an event. We all were on sprinter vans, so most of us agreed to go to the event. The others got dropped back off at the training site. Needless to say, the ex-friend's actions continued at the event. At this point, I could no longer take it and needed to address it. So, I asked her to step outside. I took the opportunity to address all of my concerns from that trip and spoke about the past. I explained why I had stopped talking to her the first time and that I wouldn't deal with those types of behaviors from her again. Of course, she claimed she didn't recall too much of those incidents. When I told her that the trainer noticed how she was blocking him from speaking to me, she tried to act as if she didn't know he was interested in me and said she wouldn't interact with him anymore unless it were about business. I then explained the Cairo situation and her attempt to withhold that information from me. Her reply was they mentioned going as a group while at the gala that I didn't attend, and she thought it was a private invite. This didn't make sense to me since I was the one connected to the network and had invited her in.

As we continued the conversation, a few trainees walked out, so we ended the discussion. We all decided to grab a quick bite to eat, but she took it in for the night. When we arrived at our location, the trainer saw me without her and asked where she was, and I explained to him that she had gone back to the hotel. I added that she was probably upset because I addressed her about the whole ordeal. I told him how she withheld the information about Cairo because she thought it was a private invite.

"That's not true," he said while looking at me.

The trainer told me that the ex-friend had sent an email to the travel agent stating that she and another girl wanted to go. The other girl's name he mentioned was her other friend. Apparently, she wanted her other friend to go with her and not me.

The following day, as we were preparing to head home, I thought to myself that it was going to be a long trip back. When I stop dealing with someone, I cease communication. I shut down and shut them off, and when it came to the ex-friend, I had nothing more to say to her.

The first thirty to forty-five minutes of our travel were

just awkward! I listened to a training session on my phone for the majority of the time. She ended up breaking the silence by asking to discuss things between us, saying we needed to talk through things if we were friends because that's how we would grow. We talked about everything that happened years ago and more recently with the current situation. During our conversation, she admitted that she had made mistakes.

She then said, "Let me ask you a question. Do you trust me?"

I chuckled and replied, "NO!"

That's when she apologized and asked me to give her another chance. I accepted her apology but still didn't feel I could trust her.

We then started talking about the upcoming investment opportunity scheduled for the next month in a different state. She informed me that she was going, and I explained I had plans to go, too. We both wanted to get started planting our seeds. Also, the trainer told us the investment entry was lower; therefore, we would not need to partner. Our conversation ended with her asking for a fresh start.

In the weeks leading up to the investment class, I texted her about the trip to Cairo. One of the main reasons was to see what her plans were regarding a hotel room since the travel agent stated the cost for single occupancy would be more than sharing a room with someone. She was vague in her reply—only saying that she was trying to go and would room with one of the trainees. I thought it was strange that she would rather share a room with someone she had just met instead of me.

Our views when it came to friendship were very different, and for that reason, I didn't feel committed to ours. Our communication didn't come to a complete halt; however, I didn't know what to say to her. As the saying goes, "Trust takes a lifetime to build and only minutes to destroy." It was hard for me to have a regular conversation with her, but I knew if we were ever going to give our friendship a fresh start, I would have to ease my way into it.

With the week of the next investment opportunity soon approaching, I wanted to see if the ex-friend would mention anything about it or suggest that we ride together as we did before, especially since we lived in the same city. Well, that Monday of the class, she sent me a text message asking for my email address. She said her friend wanted me to speak at her event. I kindly gave it to her. Other than that, there was no mention of the upcoming investment class taking place that Saturday. I didn't even know if she was going or not.

The day of the event arrived, and I hadn't heard anything from her. I left early that morning since the location was about four hours away. When I arrived at the class, I noticed she wasn't there.

Well, I guess that's why she never mentioned anything— because she wasn't coming, I thought to myself.

Later that evening, everyone from the class went to look at a few areas. We had two vans full of investors, and the trainer asked if I could ride in their van.

During the drive, the trainer looked at me and asked, "What's up with your girl? Where is she?"

When I told him that I hadn't spoken to her, he told me, "She's here, but she said she was with her family."

Looking at him with a confused expression, I replied, "Oh, you talked to her?"

He told me that she had texted him saying she was at the hotel trying to find his room. He said he didn't respond after seeing that text.

He ended the conversation about the ex-friend by saying, "I'm not entertaining her."

After riding around with the investors for a few hours, we stopped to get something to eat. The class ended late, so by the time we did stop to eat, it was almost eleven o'clock at night. Inside the restaurant, the trainer sat directly in front of me, and his assistant sat one seat over from him. Everyone else took a seat at the nearby tables.

All of a sudden, he looked down at his phone and said, "Your girl is looking for you."

He was being facetious, but he had received a text from her. I immediately had flashbacks of her calling my old guy friend's phone.

"She's not looking for me," I said while looking at him.

He reached over to show me the text that she sent asking where everyone was. Keep in mind that it was after eleven o'clock at night. She didn't want to know where everyone was; she wanted to know where he was and with who. I'm sure she hoped he would reply that he was back in his room and invite her to join him. She had no clue that I went to the class or was right there with him when she texted him. And I'm certain she didn't think he would tell me about her texting him.

She had reached out to me that Monday but didn't mention anything about going to the class. Her not letting me know she was there and then texting him in the late evening hour is where the line was drawn in the sand for me. Would a true friend do that? Would *your* friend do this? I knew then that I couldn't continue trying to have a friendship with her. I truly believe she reached out to him hoping he would entertain her that night without me knowing.

The next morning, I reached out to our mutual friend and told her that I was done with the ex-friend. After I explained what happened, she couldn't believe the ex-friend would try something like that after asking me to give our friendship another chance. I truly think she has a mental imbalance and deeply-rooted jealousy issues. There's no other way to explain why someone who calls herself a friend would do these things.

I eventually blocked her from one of my social media platforms, but she was still my Facebook friend. However, in real life, I was done trying to be friends with her and done trying to put her in a position to win. There were times I filtered my posts so that she couldn't see the helpful information I shared with my other friends. As for Cairo, I postponed the trip to invest in another project, but she still went. I'm sure she did what she does best. However, that wasn't my concern.

Prior to all of this, my spiritual advisor told me to be careful with whom I ate. I heard him, but I didn't put too much thought into it. About a year later, she blocked me from her Facebook page. I didn't block her on that platform when I blocked her from the others because I could control what she saw by using the filter option. Not to mention, I wanted her to see some parts of my come up.

All I kept thinking was, *God will prepare a table for me in the midst of my enemies.* What's so ironic is that when I reached back out to my spiritual advisor, he told me, "I don't like her energy for you. She's an opportunist. She's the type who will smile in your face and still do you dirty. She's the type who says she won't do something but will do it. It's almost like she's competing with you."

I've had the same spiritual advisor for a few years now, and he has always been on point.

If I can be honest, this situation had me very angry. Every time I would tell someone what happened, it triggered all of those old emotions. No one who had been in my life for that long had ever done the things the ex-friend did to me. It's clear to me now that she had a scarcity mindset and viewed me as competition. I sincerely wanted to put her in a position to win, but she wanted to put her own wrongful, selfish needs first and was willing to burn the bridge to someone who only wanted to help.

It is dangerous to have people around you that have a scarcity mindset and view you as competition. You have to also watch out for people who are opportunists. They will do anything to make sure they come up, even if their acts are unethical. They will only engage in relationships that benefit them. It's all about them; they can't think beyond their own needs and wishes.

As you climb higher, there will be people who want to attach to you for the wrong reasons. Learn to expel those people from your life. When someone shows you their true colors the first time, believe them. I gave the ex-friend numerous chances, but she remained the same person. Trust your intuition. If something doesn't feel right about a person, take heed to that. The thing I had to learn how to do in this situation was redirect my energy and focus on dominating my goals. I was definitely on the brink of a major financial shift when this was brewing. This clearly came as a major distraction to try to derail me from great success. I also had to understand that her behavior towards me reflected the issues she was battling beneath the surface. She was nothing like a friend but more like a frenemy.

Experiencing jealousy, envy, and betrayal can embed harmful emotions deeply into our being. Think back to a time when you may have experienced these things. If someone such as a friend, family member, or partner does these things to us, our trust in others erodes. We then have to learn how to disassociate from those memories so that we don't get stuck in a cycle and keep ourselves from progressing beyond those points. These circumstances bring about wisdom and invaluable learning lessons. We can choose to act in ways that favor or impede our personal growth.

Here are a few ways you can overcome these experiences:

1. **MEDITATION**. Meditate to wipe out the old memories or thought patterns.

2. **FORGIVE**. When I say forgive, I mean detaching yourself from the pain and frustration buried within.

3. **SLOWLY REBUILD YOUR FAITH**. Start peeling back your faith slowly. It's going to be hard at first to let people in and start trusting them. But slowly easing into it, you'll redevelop a sense of confidence in others.

4. **CUT OFF PEOPLE YOU DON'T TRUST**. You do not have to put up with untrustworthy people. This is for your well-being. Choosing to keep these people around will only lead to you distrusting everyone as a whole. Cut them off if you know they are not right for you.

5. **FIND YOUR TRIBE**. Many wonderful, honest people want to be around someone just like you. They, too, may have experienced the things you've been through and are looking to earn your trust.

6. **KEEP YOUR EMOTIONS IN CHECK**. For me, this was the hardest thing to do. In order to heal, you must check your emotions. You will remain stuck in the past if you obsess over it. Emotions are the essence of our existence, and if not controlled, they can block progress in our lives. Think logically and understand that it is in our best interest to keep moving forward.

AFFIRMATIONS:

- I am free from the wrongdoings of others.
- I am unaffected by their behavior.
- I work with others to set goals and reach accomplishments together.
- I trust in the goodwill of others, and I know kindness will prevail.

Chapter 6
Overcoming Spiritual Weakness

*"We are not human beings having a spiritual experience;
we are spiritual beings having a human experience."*
Pierre Teilhard de Chardin

Regardless of your religious or spiritual views, we are all connected. We all have the power to manifest. It is up to us to tap into the power within and open ourselves to a richer experience.

I believe having a strong why and having faith in something bigger than us will keep you going when you're facing challenges. Let's look at the why. If you're on a weight-loss journey, your why may be your health. When you're on a debt-free journey, your why may be financial freedom. I'd like for you to think about the "why" for your life's journey. Why are you here at this very moment? What are you supposed to fulfill within this lifetime? What lessons are you supposed to learn?

We are all going to face real-life human challenges that may seem hard to bear. And in those moments, we have to pull strength from a higher source. Often when life gets too hard, many people resort to all sorts of coping mechanisms, such as drugs, alcohol, and sexual addictions, to cope with reality. These are all temporary experiences that mask what needs to be dealt with internally and on a deeper level spiritually. Whatever your beliefs are, tap into that. As for me, this is a look into my journey and how I found the strength to overcome spiritual weakness.

Growing up, I always felt there was something more to life—something more than what I was learning in church at the time. I always believed in a higher power. Even at a younger age, I referred to the Creator as a higher power. I recall having a conversation with an old friend one night, while we both starred at the stars, and said there's something greater than us. I grew up in the Christian religion, so I automatically adapted to it, and I tried my best to follow that doctrine. Now, we weren't in church all the time, but we did attend on certain occasions.

When life happens to you, you have to tap into what you have known in order to cope. This held true for me when my ex passed away. One of the reasons I have always felt like there was more to what I was taught was because of my spiritual experiences. Before my first love passed away, I had a vision where I saw him in his casket. I quickly dismissed the image by thinking of something else. It was as if I feared I would think it into existence, but it happened anyway. During that moment of reality, I had to turn to something in order to cope. Thankfully, it wasn't any substances; for me, it was church.

I vividly remember calling my cousin to ask her for a church recommendation, and the spirit led her to direct me to the church where she was a member. The sermon preached by the pastor the first day I went to that church was about grieving. The message was so timely that I thought to myself, *My angels knew what I needed to hear*. I felt my footsteps were ordered.

Feeling drawn to that church, I decided to make it my church home. It helped me a great deal with what I was experiencing at that time. I would ask for confirmations, and they would be revealed through the pastor. I went to church faithfully and attended various events, revivals, and whatever else was going on. Even still, with all of that, I felt church was like a temporary high. Sundays were always like a high—filled with excitement. By the middle of the week, I needed another refill, which was fine. However, I wanted to learn how to balance my spiritual weakness without depending on a person or place.

I have always been a logical thinker. I started to think about different cultures and their beliefs. I came across something quite interesting to me when studying. It's called Sho-shin. Sho-shin is a word derived from Zen Buddhism, and it means "beginner's mind." It refers to having an attitude of openness, eagerness, and lack of preconception when studying a subject, even when learning at an advanced level, just as a beginner would. According to an article on the Wikipedia website, your religious beliefs are mostly a result of what system you were raised in—whether you agree or disagree. People raised by Christian families tend to be Christians. People raised by Muslim families tend to be Muslims. Your parent's attitudes toward religion tend to shape your attitude. The way we approach our day-to-day life results from the system we were trained in and the mentors we had along the way. At some point, we all learned to think from someone else. This is how knowledge is passed down.

Here are two questions I would like to present, though. Who is to say the way you originally learned something was the right way? What if you were taught only one way of doing things and not necessarily the best way?

This is how I thought for many years, which caused me to dig deeper and research everything with an open mind.

For me, I like church, but it was almost like elementary schooling to me. No offense. You get what you're supposed to get, apply it, and graduate to the next level. During the time I attended church, I became less religious but grew closer to the Creator. You may refer to the Creator as God, Higher Power, Most High, Buddha, Muhammad, etc. I believe different roads lead back to the same destination. I refer to the Creator as God in some instances, but the word God has become a closed concept. A mental image is created when the word God is uttered—perhaps of an old man with a white beard. But, inevitably, a male of some age or ethnicity is painted mentally.

The moment I decided to dig deeper with an open mind, I started feeling more liberated. I continued to pray, meditate, and receive confirmation messages still the same. I stopped going to church but continued my spiritual journey by praying, meditating, and studying the Bible and other spiritual materials. Even though I was on this spiritual journey without a shepherd, I found I was able to grow and handle trials on my own. I recall one of the church mothers seeing me during this time and commenting that I looked so full of joy and happiness. Truthfully, that's because I felt it. I was able to clearly see my life's purpose and find a journey that resonated with me.

Also, on this journey, I ran into a spiritual person who

told me that I had a gift of seeing things, but I suppressed it because of the fear of what others may think. What they told me was true. Being clairvoyant is often associated with evil or demonized. Some churchgoers were taught to dismiss certain things as evil, which didn't sit well with me. Some of those people are very judgmental. After that interaction, I decided to speak with one of my aunts about what I experienced, and she said those spiritual gifts ran heavily on that side of the family. She explained that my great-grandmother was a seer and could see things before they happened. My aunt also has gifts and many other family members on that side of the family. I, however, feel they suppress them because of religion. My great-grandmother even came to me in a dream with a message. I was curious about it, so I reached out to a few members on Facebook. I asked why the message came to me and not the other members, and they said it was probably because I was more aware.

I could go into a lot of experiences, but I don't want to stray from the topic. There were certain things I needed answers to that I couldn't get with the current teachings of religion, so I sought after more. However, I do believe everyone is at different stages spiritually; I totally get it. On this quest to fulfill what I was missing, I overcame my spiritual weakness and emotions around grief. I still have my days where I get emotional from missing my ex's physical form, but that's human nature. Overall, my understanding of life, death, and everything in between has been put into a higher perspective. I'm at total peace with this understanding.

This all started back in 2013. That's when I had a major download of sorts. At this same time, I had downloads about changing my mindset and habits about my finances. I took heed to that download, and my life has been on the rise ever since. Doors have been opening, and manifestations have come to fruition.

Being balanced spiritually has allowed me to handle my challenges on this journey. I now look for deeper meanings behind the things that I encounter. I pull strength in knowing that at the end of it all, this is an experience. Your spirit is in your body to experience life. How amazing is that?

I was finally able to tap into what I have been trying to figure out my entire life. The more I gravitated towards figuring things out, the more things were revealed, and everything revealed helped me overcome spiritual weakness. We all encounter spiritual weakness, but you can overcome it by growing closer to the Creator. Seek a deeper understanding in areas that are unclear, and do whatever feels right. Tap into what resonates with you.

I would encourage you to work on your spiritual health to help you navigate your human experience. Pray and ask for clarity in your direction. Have faith that whatever direction you are guided will serve a purpose. Don't allow anything to be forced upon you. If it doesn't feel right, then it's not right for you. Learn to respect everyone's views, even if they are different from your own.

This is your spiritual journey, and on this journey, you will have to rely on a higher power to help you overcome the challenges in order to have a richer life experience.

Chapter 7
Overcoming Financial Challenges

Financial challenges happen to everyone at some point, causing anxiety. However, realizing that there is always a way out can help ease the feeling of financial stress. As we go through these financial phases, it's best to remember what these situations felt like, and more importantly, how to be better prepared in the future.

In 2017, I co-authored a book titled *I Hate Being Broke.* My chapter touched briefly on my journey and talked about ways to get out of debt and regain financial control. I'll elaborate more in this chapter about how I overcame my financial challenges. I'll also provide applicable steps you can use.

Growing up, I watched my granddad, who was in the

military, and my grandmother, who had multiple jobs, work hard to obtain things in life. I can honestly say I didn't have to want for anything. Even with getting what I wanted, I always wanted to strive for more independently. I believed in working to get what I wanted and not relying on anyone else to give it to me.

Before leaving Elizabeth City, I remember watching my grandmother cut up credit cards while saying, "Don't get yourself into this trouble." Those memories stuck with me throughout the early part of my adult years. Believe it or not, our past—whether positive or not—is what shapes our belief system. It's what we learn through those experiences that mold our future. Most of us learned about finances through our parents or peers. Then we act on that based on their level of knowledge.

When I first moved to Greensboro, after securing a job, I rented out a space on my aunt's couch. At that time, she had a one-bedroom apartment. I don't believe in adding extra burdens on anyone, so I agreed to pay her for allowing me to live there. During this time, I mapped out my goals, determined to stay the course. My first goal was to get my own apartment and furniture. I worked a lot of overtime and ate Ramen noodles in order to aggressively attack my goals. Within a few months, I had accomplished them and was living on my own.

I have always been a saver and a good steward over my

money. I'm not sure where these behaviors come from and sometimes jokingly say it's my sixth sense. However, as good as I thought I was with money, I soon realized you don't know what you don't know.

By 2004, I had landed a job at a Fortune 500 company, completed cosmetology school, and purchased a new car. Life was great, and so was my income. I even put off going to the cosmetology board because I was comfortable with my income. I was making more than my peers who had degrees. There were times when I sent checks to my grandparents as a token of my appreciation. It felt good to be able to give back.

This company had great benefits, and the people there became like family. I remember one of my trainers telling me to open up a 401(k) and start putting money aside. She gave me a lot of advice early on and told me that I would be rich one day. Still holding onto what my grandmother said about credit cards, I was still using cash and debit cards during my financial journey. My friends and family tried to encourage me to get a credit card to help build up my credit score. They suggested I needed at least one credit card for emergencies, and for the longest time, I resisted.

In 2006, our company offered us applications for a new credit card. Biting the bullet, I decided to apply, intending on only using it for emergencies. My focus was not to fall into credit card debt and mess up my credit.

I had just purchased a brand-new car two years before and made a New Year's resolution to pay it off at the beginning of 2006. I bought my car at a 4.25% interest rate, at 72 months, with payments of $288. My starting balance was $11,366.88. I was able to make double and sometimes triple payments by working overtime until I paid it off. In total, it took me two years and ten months to pay my car off. I was so excited that I called home to tell my grandparents. I remember my granddad saying, "You said you were going to do it."

Even though I was responsible with my money, I also had some careless spending moments. For instance, I couldn't tell you how much gas cost. I just knew I had enough money in my account, so the cost wasn't my concern. There were times when I did this at the shopping malls, too. I wouldn't look at the price tag. I would just buy whatever I wanted, knowing the money was available. Clearly, the word budget wasn't a part of my lexicon.

As we make more money, it's a habit to want to spend more. I managed to save money, but there was no specific amount I had planned for a particular purpose. My bills were paid, I had spending money, and I put a little away. I thought that was good enough.

With my car paid off, I started thinking about building my first home. I had a high credit score, a savings account, investments, and no debt. The time seemed perfect. In 2017, one of my other aunts and I were talking, and I shared with her that I was thinking about buying a home. She told me there was a new subdivision close to where she lived that we could check out.

One Saturday evening, we decided to go and take a look. The agent on duty took down my information and took us around to look at what was called "Spec Homes." These homes were already built and move-in ready. I also had the option to build and customize my own. I told the agent I wanted a three-bedroom house with a brick front. When we began to talk numbers, she recommended I check out a particular model home nearby in another subdivision that was more in my price range. Upon entering the house, I had a feeling this model type was going to be the one. It was a perfect starter home for me.

Before I knew it, I was signing papers in her office and pre-approved to purchase my first home. It was exciting yet scary because I would now be responsible for paying a 30-year mortgage! A plethora of thoughts ran through my mind—one being, "What if I can't pay the mortgage due to a job loss?" Even with those "what ifs" running rapidly through my mind, I still went for it. This home matched the one I had dreamt about for so long.

In January 2008, I closed on my first home. The feeling was indescribable. I had achieved something else I had set out to accomplish.

On the day of closing, I went furniture shopping, and because I had a great credit score, I was able to furnish nearly my whole home—all except one room. I had a "No money down, and no interest for two years" option. The plan was to pay off the balance quickly like I did with my car. What was the problem with this? I was counting money that hadn't come yet. Indeed, it was a valuable lesson of what not to do.

At the end of 2008, I had to face one of my biggest fears. The economy took a turn, and my company ended up making job cuts. Unfortunately, I was one of the casualties. I quickly started applying to other companies, and luckily, I had two job offers within a couple of months. One of the companies was similar to the last company where I worked, and the other company was a different career field. After weighing the pros and cons of each company, I decided to go with the company that was different from my last. It proved to be the best decision since I received word later that the other company had closed down. Even though I was thankful to have another job, I wasn't entirely out of the woods yet because my income was nearly cut in half.

The year was 2009, and I had just started the new job. Now I had to figure out how to manage the same bills with the new income. While in training, the first thing I recall doing was looking for a testing site to get my cosmetology license. It had been five years since I finished school. Back then, I was comfortable with the amount of money I was making, so I put off getting my cosmetology license. I knew now I needed to secure my plan B. I never again wanted to be in a position where I had to worry about my income if Corporate America decided to pull the rug from underneath me.

After studying every day after work until I felt comfortable enough to take the test, I finally scheduled a day to go in. There are two tests you have to pass for cosmetology: Theory and Practical. I took the Theory test first.

As I walked into the testing site, my anxiety level shot through the roof. I gave the receptionist my name and ID, then proceeded to the testing area. When I sat down at the computer, I said a quick prayer and went for it. After completing the test, I sat there anxiously waiting for my test score. After what seemed like an eternity, the lady came into the room, handed me a piece of paper, and said, "Congratulations! You passed!" My excitement caused me to be nearly speechless. I was so proud of myself. A couple of weeks later, I took the practical exam. I received those scores by mail and passed that, too. I now had a sense of security and another goal checked off of my list.

As time went by, I figured out how to manage my mortgage and bills, but now I had debt from the furniture company due. Things began to get a little tight. I started pulling from my savings account, 401(k), and cashed out my Certificate of Deposit (CD), all to stay afloat. Even though things were tight, I paid everyone on time. My credit score was rising, but my savings was steadily depleting.

After draining my accounts, I started relying on my credit card to pay for food and gas. I was literally living paycheck to paycheck. At this point, I found myself digging a deep financial hole at a fast pace.

I worked at the salon part-time but soon left the establishment because the employees weren't getting paid on time or were shorted on our commission totals. By the recommendation of my aunt, I called my bank to ask for a mortgage reduction. She had some assistance with her home, so I decided to give it a try.

After contacting the bank, I explained to them the situation with my job, and they told me there was nothing they could do because of the type of loan I had. I didn't qualify for the Harp Program, which most people were getting back then. Apparently, the type of loan I had was not backed by Fannie Mae or Freddie Mac. When I called my aunt to tell her that I didn't qualify, she asked if I was making my payments on time each month, and I told her yes. She then said, "They're not going to help you because you're paying every month." She then advised me to miss a payment on purpose to see if that would help. So, the next month, I withdrew the amount of my mortgage out of my bank account, put it in an envelope, and stashed it in my top drawer.

The following month rolled around, and I called the bank again. Once again, they denied the request. Now I had late fees and took a hit on my credit. This was all bad. At this point, I just took the money from my drawer and paid the past due amount.

A few months later, someone told me about a forbearance option they received and suggested I try that. They told me to visit a local credit counseling service first to have them draft out my income and expenses, then provide that information to my bank. I jumped right on it, and guess what? It worked—well, for a short amount of time.

All of this was new to me, so I didn't know what I was doing. The way the forbearance worked was they allowed me to pay about $350 less a month, but it was a second lien on the property. After finding this out, I canceled that option.

The whole situation turned out to be very messy. I mean, I had money to pay my mortgage, but after I finished paying all of my bills, I had to resort to putting things on credit to make it to the next payday.

Fast forward to the year 2013, which I call my

turnaround year. This was when things shifted in my life for the better. At the beginning of that year, I was shopping and traveling to mask my reality. My debt was growing, and my income was stagnant. I was accustomed to a certain lifestyle and didn't properly adjust when things got tight. I would say I was on vacation, but I was "tripping" literally.

In April of that year, I flew out to L.A., and in June of that year, I was in Puerto Rico. I remember posting the details of the trips on Facebook. From the outside looking in, one would think I had it all together. In fact, I was at Wal-Mart one evening and ran into an old coworker. She looked at me and asked, "How can I get on because you are doing it?" I smiled and gave some encouraging words, but my financial situation told a different story behind closed doors.

In August 2013, my friend and I took a road trip to Atlanta to attend a hair show. While visiting, we stopped to support two of the local celebrities' boutiques. One I took a picture with at the checkout counter. Little did I know that picture would be the start of something great.

As I sat in the car outside of a restaurant, I felt as though I had a download of some sort during this trip. I captured a picture of myself in that moment and posted it on Facebook with a deep caption. I knew something had to change, and that day, it all clicked. I started thinking about all of the fun I had that year on my trips but also recalled how I felt as soon as I returned home. It was as if a gray cloud was lingering over my head. The trips were nothing more than temporary highs.

When I returned home from Atlanta, I remember thinking I had to do something immediately to turn my financial situation around. Still playing in my head what my old coworker had said to me in Wal-Mart, I felt like my life was just smoke and mirrors, and I didn't like that. I didn't want to portray a false image of having it all together when in fact, I didn't. In *our* community, our people would rather look like they have money than actually having it. I was no longer about that lifestyle.

The first thing I had to do was face the numbers head-on. I had to identify the problem and make adjustments. I decided to cut back where I could and bring in additional income. I called the salon owner, asking if I could start back working at the salon again. This time, however, I had a plan. I also stayed on top of my commissions to avoid confusion with payout. Even with these adjustments, I felt like it wasn't enough. I wanted to challenge myself. As I sat in deep thought, an idea came to me—cut out shopping. I told myself that I wasn't going to go shopping for an entire year.

Now THAT was a challenge. I gladly accepted it and quickly created a countdown calendar to track my progress. I started the challenge on August 17, 2013, and immediately took to social media with my countdown timer to make everyone aware of what I was doing.

During this no-spend challenge, I stopped dining out and traveling. My friend was going on a business trip to the Virgin Islands and asked me to go, but I had to decline. She understood my plan and went without me. That same friend had a hotel party for her birthday. I was somewhat prepared for that, but she decided to make it a pool party the day of. Well, I didn't have a swimsuit packed, nor could I buy one because of this challenge. I wasn't about to cheat myself to get one, and that's exactly what I told her. It all worked out because my cousin had an extra swimsuit.

That same weekend, my flip-flops popped. Jokingly, my friend said, "Girl, you're not going to get a new pair? You're just going to walk around like that?" I laughed and told her that I would figure it out. Luckily, my aunt let me use her flip-flops. This wasn't the first time I received comments about my footwear. While working at the salon, I had holes in my shoes. The girls there would laugh and joke about it, but they also knew about my challenge. I was fully committed to it. Remember when I said I would rather look like I don't have money and have it than look like I have money and not have it. On the outside looking in, I'm sure it looked like I was broke.

When the holidays came around, I had to closet shop. I was so used to going to the mall and getting something new for each occasion. As far as gift shopping for others, I redeemed my credit card reward points and purchased gift certificates. By this time, I had made great progress and wasn't living paycheck to paycheck any longer.

Every couple of months, I would post an update, and before I knew it, I had completed my 365-Day No-Spend Challenge. Because of this, my movement went viral. I even did a few interviews about it. My first interview was on the Debt-Free Divas podcast, and my second interview was with *Forbes*. *FORBES*?! Yes, *Forbes*! Here I am, a woman from a small city who had big dreams and ended up featured in *Forbes Magazine*. I believe in the Law of Attraction and speaking things with intention into the universe. A couple of years earlier, I had posted on Facebook a mock photo using an app on my phone of me on the cover of *Forbes Magazine*. Can you believe my Forbes feature and that mockup I posted online had the same pose?! I had to do a double-take when that vision came to fruition. I didn't know how it would happen; I just believed it could.

I want you to know there's nothing special about me. I just decided to do something different by sacrificing temporality to get different results. If you're going through financial challenges right now, I want you to face your issues head-on. Make a commitment to turn your life around immediately. Don't worry about what people may think; worry about getting your financial house in order. I promise you it's so worth it.

When I decided to open up online about my journey, I found out many people were struggling financially. They would inbox me for advice and help. I can tell you this—you would never know some of these people had any issues. They looked like they had everything well put together. I remember speaking in Atlanta at an event about finances, and I had a general conversation with a young lady. She had a lot of social media followers and had recently posted a picture of a new BMW. When I asked her did she have an emergency fund or a retirement account in place, she told me no. At that moment, I realized our culture needed help. This is why I decided to become a Certified Financial Educator and created a series of courses and e-books to help.

We have to kill this self-gratifying ego of wanting to look like we have money. We are the only race of people who feel the need to prove our financial status by buying cars, clothes, jewelry, etc.

With financial challenges comes financial stress. Money is one of the biggest causes of chronic stress. The vast majority of people worry about their financial situation daily. If you're feeling overwhelmed by your finances, there are resources. I'll tell you exactly what I did to pull myself out of debt and regain financial control.

FINANCIAL GAME PLAN

One of the hardest things to do sometimes is to check yourself. But when you're sick and tired of being sick and tired, you'll make the necessary changes. We change our behavior when the pain of staying the same becomes greater than the pain of changing. At this point, forget what others may think. Your reality is more important than their perception.

The first step is to identify that there is a problem. You can continue to mask the issue, but the problem will still exist. Yes, facing the issue can be overwhelming or intimidating, but the faster you tackle it, the freer you'll be. It is important to determine your WHY, which will keep you going when you want to give up. Your overall attitude towards financial freedom can determine your trajectory. For me, I wanted to experience true financial freedom. I could no longer live my life living paycheck to paycheck. So, I sat down, pulled my financials, and devised a plan, moving with a sense of urgency. Once you know where you stand, you can take massive action.

Starting the actual phase of financially getting back on track will require you to determine your cash flow. Your income minus your expenses determine your cash flow number. Write out how much income you bring in monthly. Cash inflow can include salaries, interest from savings, interest from investments, or dividends from investments. If your monthly income varies, use an average calculation. Next, determine your expenses to subtract from your income. Your cash outflow can include rent/mortgage, utility bills, grocery, gas, etc. This will give you a snapshot of your cash flow.

Pull a copy of your bank statement from last month, and take a look at what you spent money on the most. In most of my clients' cases, it was eating out and shopping. Add up those numbers so you can see how much money you're wasting monthly. We have to be mindful of our spending.

FREEING UP CASH

Once you know what your cash flow looks like and have taken a look at where you frequently spend money, now it's time to make some adjustments Ladies, if you're getting your nails done every two weeks at the cost of around $25, that's a total of $600 per year. My nails had to go! When it comes to getting your hair done, be creative and figure out some cost-effective measures. I'm a hairstylist, so for me, this was easy. Men, budget accordingly for your grooming.

Cut the Cord

The next thing that had to go for me was cable television. If you're trying to pay down debt or save up some cash, it might be time to cut the cord. Consider alternatives such as:

- Hulu ($5.99/month)
- Netflix ($12.99/month)
- Amazon Instant Video ($12.99/a month)
- Fire TV Stick (One-time payment of $34.00)
- HD Antenna (One-time payment of $6.00)

This is a switch you can make right away. Even if the switch is only temporary, it still beats paying extra right now while you're trying to get financially fit. Remember, short-term sacrifices for long-term gain.

Creditors

Next, free up cash by checking with your creditors. Make a list of all of your credit card companies. Then contact each one and ask them if you are eligible for a lower interest rate. Periodically, credit card companies review your accounts for lower rates, but in most cases, you'll never know you qualify. Do this for every card you have. This will help you save on interest paid monthly.

If you don't qualify for a lower interest rate, check if you can do a balance transfer to a lower interest rate credit card. Be careful with balance transfer fees, though. On average, transfer fees can be 3%. Factor that in when determining if it makes sense to transfer your balance. Magnifymoney.com is a website you can check out. This site allows you to search for the best balance transfer rates. It'll also tell you which ones have a 0% transfer fee. Try not to use your cards at this point. The main objective is to save on interest and pay off the balance.

Cell Phone

Another thing I did to save money was call my cell phone provider. It's a good idea to check your current plan and make adjustments. You may have to switch providers, or there might be certain discounts for which you may be eligible. If you have an employer, check your corporate discounts; my company had discounts with several providers. Also, check with your local credit unions. I used a corporate discount to save on my monthly bill.

Auto Insurance

Save money on collision and comprehensive coverage by raising your deductible—the amount the insurance company doesn't cover for repairs. For example, if the repair bill is $2,000, and you have a $500 deductible, the insurer will pay out $1,500. You can also switch auto insurance companies for a lower rate. Did you know you can shop for new auto coverage every six or twelve months? I was able to switch and save $340. I had been with my old auto insurance company for over 20 years! When their rates started increasing, it prompted me to look elsewhere. Everquote.com is a site you can use to compare auto insurance rates. I was able to switch online hassle-free. That website simplifies your process by pulling quotes from different carriers, and it's free to use. Also, if you're a homeowner, check with them about discounted bundle rates if you get your home insurance through them.

Those are just a couple of things that can help you free up some cash. Think about other ways you can cut back. Maybe cancel that gym membership you don't use. Brainstorm and cut back as much as you can.

BRING IN EXTRA INCOME

Once you've found ways to free up extra cash and you have cut back as much as you can, it's time to find ways to bring in additional income. Here are a few things that can help:

- **Sell your stuff.** By selling things you no longer need, you remove clutter from your home and profit in the process. Sell your gently used items at consignment stores or utilize online platforms like Craigslist, OfferUp, or Facebook Marketplace.

- **Become a service provider.** What services could you provide that can bring in additional income? Do you teach? Are you an animal lover? Are small children your favorite people to be around? You can earn extra income by tutoring, walking dogs, house sitting, or babysitting. If you have special skills, you can freelance to bring in additional revenue, from writing and design to coding and administrative work. There is a huge demand for freelancers. Post your services on websites like Upwork.com and Fiverr.com. You can also teach classes locally or online and charge a small fee. You can write a book and self-publish it. I have taught several clients how to make money online with my Digital Slay masterclass. You can sign-up for it on my website Ahfinancialgroup.com.

- **Start an online business.** There are many opportunities to start an online business, and it's easy to do. You can become an affiliate marketer and do vlogs about products and services you love. Blog and make money from advertisements. Start an online store or boutique. Use social media to your advantage.

- **Get a part-time job.** Find something that works with your current schedule and apply. Use the income from this job to get ahead.

Opportunities are all around you. Choose one that seems most interesting and start adding to your income.

Budgeting

Once you have found ways to decrease your expenses and bring in extra income, you need a money plan. It is so essential to arrange your financial priorities in life. Doing so will help to secure your financial future. Priorities lead to prosperity.

A budget is a spending plan for your money. Creating this spending plan allows you to determine in advance whether you will have enough money to do the things you need to do or like to do.

The first step to creating your budget is to find a system you will use consistently. It's not enough to create a spending plan and then never look at it again. Budget systems range from grabbing a pencil and some paper (which is my method of choice), using online templates, and budgeting or accounting software. There are also apps you can use, such as Mint.com and Everydollar.com. Of course, there are plenty of others.

Once you determine your method, it's time to apply your numbers. Here's a guideline for the recommended budget percentage. Multiply your monthly income by these recommended percentages to see how you rank. Note: percentages may vary depending on your state.

- Housing – 30%
- Utilities – 10%
- Food – 10%
- Transportation – 10%
- Medical – 5%
- Recreation – 5%
- Debt – 5%
- Personal – 10%
- Savings/Investing – 15%

Use this reference as an example and tweak it as needed. The main goal is to have a plan for your money and not overextend yourself to where you are living paycheck to paycheck. Housing will take up the largest part of your income. I would say to stay under 35% of your total monthly income. You don't want to be house poor.

Budgeting for Inconsistent Income

Here are some budgeting tips for those who have

inconsistent income. Sure, it's easy to budget when you expect the same amount every month. However, budgeting may be a little harder for people who work on commission and those who are self-employed.

- **Step 1:** Determine what you expect to bring home for the month. If you aren't sure, use last year's lowest month as your starting point.
- **Step 2:** Figure out exactly how much money is needed each month to cover your four walls: food, clothing, shelter, and transportation.

As your income comes in, you'll pay down the list in step 2. Next, prioritize the following in step 3.

- **Step 3:** Remaining dollars should go towards irregular expenses. Examples of irregular expenses are savings, debts, medical bills, entertainment, etc.
- **Step 4:** As your money comes in, you'll pay down the above list in order. If more money comes in, figure out where it goes on your list. If less money comes in, figure out what you can cut back on or be okay with cutting. Remember, a budget isn't created to deprive yourself; a budget is created to keep you in check.

<u>Buffer Account & Dual Bank Method</u>

Here are a few things that helped me with staying on track with my budget. The first was having a buffer account, and the second was utilizing the dual bank account method.

What is a buffer account? A buffer account is a savings account for expenses that come up yearly. I say all the time that birthdays and holidays are no surprises. These events occur every year. The top three categories most people need a buffer account for are:

1. Vacations
2. Car Maintenance
3. Holidays and birthdays

A buffer account is not your emergency fund. This account is only for budgeting for yearly expenses. So how does a buffer account work? Let's take a look at these examples:

- **Example 1: Vacations** – Let's say today is January 1st, and you are planning a trip for July that will cost you $1,500. You have 7 months to save up the money. ($1,500 ÷ 7(months) = $214) Therefore, you will need to set aside $214 every month, including January.

- **Example 2: Holidays** – It's January 1st, and you want to have $1,000 saved up to spend on Christmas. ($1,000 ÷ 12(months) = $83) You will set aside $83 every month to meet your goal.

- **Example 3: Car Maintenance** – The amount to save in this category should be based on the total you spent on car maintenance expenses the previous year. Let's say your car taxes, registration, and oil changes totaled $1,200. ($1,200 ÷ 12(months) = $100) You should be setting aside $100 monthly.

Finally, add the total from all categories. In the above example, you will set aside $100 for car maintenance, $83 for Christmas, and $214 for vacation, totaling $397. You should transfer this amount into a savings account each month. This way, you won't have to scramble around to scrape up money when these things come up because the cash will already be in your account. Do this consistently, and your finances will change drastically.

Dual Bank Account Method

Now, let's break down the dual bank account method, which will help you stay organized when budgeting. Saving all your money in one account is a recipe for financial disaster because all of your dollars are co-mingling.

Open two bank accounts at separate establishments—each with a savings and checking account. Make sure to choose banks that offer free checking. I currently use two different credit unions. If, for some reason, you are not able to join a credit union, research some banks that offer great interest rates. Magnifymoney.com provides a list of good banks and credit unions to use.

Your primary bank account setup should look like this:

Checking account
- Main direct deposit
- Bill payment account
- Leave the debit card at home

Savings account
- Your buffer account totals are deposited into this account. (Tip: determine your buffer account amount and transfer that money from your checking to this savings account just as if you are paying a bill.)

Your secondary bank account set up should look like this:

Checking account
- Used for expenditures other than bills. Example: gas, grocery, dining out, travel, and splurge account. (Set up a specific dollar amount for each category.)

- Add up each total and deposit that amount into your checking. If you have direct deposit, have that set amount automatically transferred from your check into this checking account.

Savings account
- Emergency fund
- Miscellaneous savings

Note: You can consider moving your emergency fund from this savings account into a money market account or high-yield savings account for better interest.

By separating your expenses, you will be in better control of your finances. As stated, these methods helped me tremendously. If you lack discipline when it comes to swiping your debit card, consider using the envelope system. With this method, you take cash out of your bank account and place a certain amount into an envelope for each category.

Having a spending plan reveals waste, directs priorities, creates new habits, and reduces stress. Make it a goal this week to follow the steps in this section.

Escaping the Debt Matrix

Eliminating my debt was a priority, and I knew that I needed a solid plan to make that happen. In the beginning, every time I tried to get out of debt, it seemed like something would always come up and keep me in a perpetual cycle. I can say that I didn't have a working budget to keep track of everything. I also didn't have a system to follow for debt elimination. The following format is what I used to escape the debt matrix.

Step 1 – Secure a starter emergency fund

You need an emergency fund! Surely, you've heard this before. The question is, have you acted on that advice? About one-third of Americans haven't, and as a result, they don't have sufficient savings to pay for unexpected expenses. If you don't have an emergency fund and are hit with any unforeseen event, you will likely be forced to rely on credit cards like I did.

Aim to save $1,000 fast! If you make less than $20,000 per year, you should aim to save $500. If you have a family of four or more, aim to save $2,000. Saving this initial amount is important because it teaches you how to prepare for the unknown.

Also, keep your emergency fund liquid. Meaning, don't tie this money up in stocks or anywhere you can't cash out instantly. Open a money market or a high-yield savings account. These are some safe vehicles, and they have better interest rates than regular savings, as I mentioned before. My emergency fund is split between a money market account with my credit union and an American Express high-yield savings account. Check out Bankrate.com for a list of financial institutions that have the best high-yield saving account rates.

Remember earlier when I listed ways for you to free up extra cash and make more money? Use that extra money to put towards your emergency fund.

Step 2 – Debt eliminator

If you are currently behind with any creditors, work toward becoming current with those accounts as soon as possible by applying the debt eliminator strategy.

- List all of your debts, including medical bills, from the smallest to the largest balance. This is about quick wins and momentum. Do not be concerned with the interest rates unless you have two debts with similar payoff amounts. In that case, list the debt with the higher interest rate first. Only pay off a larger debt if it is of urgency, such as owing the IRS or if you are facing foreclosure. Otherwise, follow the format. First, focus on eliminating consumer debt (credit cards, personal bank loans, car loans, medical bills). Exclude student loans and mortgage balances from this step.

- Make the minimum payment due on all accounts with the exception of the first debt; pay as much as you can on that first debt. When the first debt is paid in full, take the amount you were paying on that account and add it to the minimum payment for the second account. Then repeat.

EXAMPLE

Auction Debt Eliminator

Creditor	Total Debt	Regular Payment	Regular + Extra Payment	New Payment
Target account	$450	$25	25+200	$225
Shell account	$600	$40	40+225	$265
Master Card account	$850	$75	75+265	$340
Parent loan	$1,200	$150	150+340	$490
Car loan	$8,000	$350	350+490	$840

Step 3 – Fully-Funded Emergency Fund

What would it take for you to live three to six months if you lost your income? A fully-funded emergency fund covers three to six months of expenses. Seventy percent of us will have a major emergency within the next ten years. It's not *if* an emergency will happen, but *when* it will happen. Credit cards are not emergency funds. You have to plan properly so you are not thrown back into a debt cycle.

By now, you should know the total of your monthly expenses. To calculate the amount needed for your fully-funded emergency fund, take the sum of your living expenses and multiply it by three or six. That's the maximum amount you should have saved in your account. Emergency accounts usually range from $5,000 to $25,000.

Step 4 – Invest

Once you have a fully-funded emergency fund and your consumer debt is paid, start some light investing. The goal is to invest at least 15% of your income. You can choose to invest in a variety of ways. Here are a few options:

- Contribute to a 401(k) plan or any other company-sponsored plan. Also, you can open an Individual Retirement Account (IRA). Check with your local bank and other online platforms to set these up.
- Invest in stocks with modern-day apps like Robinhood and Acorns. Robinhood is a free platform that allows you to choose what stock you want to invest in. You also earn up to $500 in free stock by referring others. Acorn charges $1 per month; this platform is great for beginners. You can contribute whatever amount you want and how often you want. It'll auto-invest for you based on your goals.

- Get started in real estate to accelerate your retirement goals. (I'll discuss this in more detail in the next chapter.)

Once your investments start to grow, you can tackle your student loans and mortgage.

Within seven months of following these steps, I was back on track financially. You have to get to the point where you want better for your life. In order to create the lifestyle you deserve, you are going to have to sacrifice. Set your financial priorities, determine your needs versus wants, and be disciplined when it comes to instant gratification. To get different results, you're going to have to do different, and the more you prolong getting started, the longer you'll be in the same situation. Trust me, the sacrifices I've made to get to where I am were worth it. The feeling is of great relief, and guess what? You can experience this, too. It all starts with a decision.

Chapter 8
Barriers to Creating Wealth

"Mediocrity doesn't just happen; it's chosen over time."

Todd Henry

Mediocrity

We are creatures of comfort. It's easy to get comfortable with your surroundings and even your income level. The problem with this is, being comfortable can stop us from pushing ourselves to be the best we can be. Then, in that moment, you hit a plateau and become stagnant.

To overcome mediocrity, there has to be a mental shift from conventional and societal ways of thinking. In many ways, these shifts require you to unlearn the negative and sabotaging programming you have learned from your peers, school, or throughout your adulthood in general. The foundation of the first mental shift is the power of choice. You have to take responsibility for your choices in order to pull yourself from mediocrity to a more prosperous life. No more playing victim to external circumstances; no more blaming others for any lack on your part.

The foundation of the second mental shift is transcending your independence. This happens when your thinking stretches far beyond yourself. It will require you to build your network or find a tribe that will help you bring your ideas to life.

<u>Your Network</u>

One of the critical components of my journey was being around next-level and like-minded people. I made it a priority to seek out and connect with individuals who looked like my future and not my past. I wanted to be around goal-driven people.

One evening while working at the salon, a gentleman named Joe Dudley came in to get his haircut. During his visit, he stopped near a group of stylists and started talking about a book. In passing, I overheard him say, "Have you heard of the book called *Think and Grow Rich*?" I immediately stopped to listen and then chimed in. When I told him that I had the book, he looked at me and said,

"You're invited to our weekly meetings. We are reading that book." This was perfect for me because I hadn't yet finished the book. I was elated about his invitation, and here's why.

Mr. Joe Dudley is a living legend. He is one of the world's most sought-after entrepreneurial masterminds. He's the president of Dudley Products. In 1957, he invested $10 in a Fuller Products sales kit, which later made him a millionaire at a young age. He is so much more than a successful entrepreneur, though. He is known nationally and internationally as an inspirational speaker and humanitarian who spends his time giving back to the community. He has been the recipient of numerous awards. Here are a few:

- President George Bush's 467th Point of Light Award for Dudley Fellows and Ladies Program
- Maya Angelou Tribute to Achievement Award
- Inducted into the DSA Hall of Fame with other iconic greats, including the late Nelson Mandela

So, as you can see, being invited to his home to read and network was truly an honor. I remember telling him my plans for getting out of debt and how I was currently on a no-spend challenge to accelerate my goals. I was excited and couldn't wait for their next meetup.

At the first meeting, everyone sat at a long table in the

dining room. The protocol was to read for one hour, and at the end of that hour, we would discuss the takeaways from that chapter. The chapter we were reading at that time was titled "Desire." In this chapter, it talked about transmuting desire into its financial equivalent, which consisted of these six definite practical steps:

- **Step One** – Fix in your mind the exact amount of money you desire.
- **Step Two** – Determine exactly what you intend to give in return for the money you desire.
- **Step Three** – Establish a definite date when you intend to possess the money you desire.
- **Step Four** – Create a definite plan for carrying out your desire and begin at once, whether you are ready or not, to put this plan into action.
- **Step Five** – Write out a clear, concise statement of the amount of money you intend to acquire. Name the time limit for its acquisition, state what you intend to give in return for the money, and describe clearly the plan through which you intend to accumulate it.
- **Step Six** – Read your written statement aloud, twice daily, once just before retiring at night, and once after rising in the morning. As you read, see and feel and believe yourself already in possession of the money.

I implemented those steps as indicated and produced my results. Once my no-spend challenge was over, and I had that exact amount I wrote down in my bank account, and my debt was cleared, I told Mr. Dudley when he came in the salon one weekend. It felt good sharing my story with him. Every so often, when I attended the meetings, he would tell the other individuals how excited he was about my accomplishments. I was even asked to speak at Mr. Dudley's International Business Expo in 2015.

Mr. Dudley also inspired me to write this book. When he told me to get my story out, I started writing my book but paused so many times during the process. At one point, I asked his thoughts about a ghostwriter. He responded that he wrote his book himself and that I could do it. You see, surrounding myself with like-minded people gave me that extra push and accountability on my journey. I knew I could share my goals with the members of this network and receive the support and encouragement I needed. This is why establishing a great network is important. Being surrounded by such an awesome network has opened up many doors. One thing I admired about this group was that it was predominantly blacks that attended. They all came together to learn from a millionaire how to create wealth.

So, my challenge to you is to upgrade your relationships. Get out and connect with next-level people.

WEALTH GAP

Let's talk wealth, which is the difference between what families own (a house, business, retirement savings, bank accounts, etc.) minus what they owe in mortgage, credit cards, and student loans.

Historically, African Americans lag behind whites, who have long benefited from capital extracted from Black labor and culture. At the median, non-retired African Americans in 2016 had $13,460 compared to white's median wealth, which was $142,180. The wealth gap widened back in the years 2007 to 2009 because of the recession. African Americans' wealth fell because their wealth was more concentrated in home equity. They had fewer financial reserves outside of their homes than whites did. This is also why I speak about having an emergency fund.

The current racial wealth gap stems from many decades of racial inequality from post-emancipation barriers, such as segregation in housing and schools to decimation in the workforce and redlining. Redlining is defined as a discriminatory practice by which banks and insurance companies refuse or limit loans, mortgages, insurance, etc., within specific geographic areas, especially inner-city neighborhoods. This reduced the capital in Black communities.

Research has also indicated that differences in savings

rates, inheritances, and return on investments have all been suspected of playing a significant role in maintaining the racial gap. Various things have to happen to shorten the wealth gap. Right now, we can start with the basics—financial education. The schools need to have curriculums on financial literacy. As adults, we also need to learn proper money management skills, be mindful of our spending habits, and learn how to get better returns with different asset allocation classes. In addition to these things, we must learn how to maintain and protect our wealth for generations to come.

SPENDING HABITS

"It's not your salary that makes you rich; it's your spending habit."

Charles Jaffe

According to the state of working America, Blacks spend four percent more money annually than any other race despite being the least represented race and living in poverty at the highest rate. It is reported that Blacks' spending power is $1.2 trillion annually.

We have to control our spending in order to create wealth, individually as well as a culture. Generally speaking, we have to stop that "living for the moment" mindset regarding our money. A common scenario for some of us is when we get a "large" chunk of cash or a tax refund check; we tend to splurge. We are leaking out money as a community. The Black dollar circulates in the Black community 6 hours compared to circulating a month in the Asian community, approximately 20 days in the Jewish community, and 17 days in the white community. Now, I can understand wanting things, but there's a way to go about obtaining them. Often, if we didn't have certain things growing up, we feel a sense of entitlement to buy those things for our children and ourselves without understanding things on a more logical level. Some of our people are purchasing strictly for admiration.

The curators of the *Dopeness Blog* had this to say: "Black people tend to spend money on fashion. Black people get made fun of for not having on the newest pair of Jordans sneakers or brand name-brand shirt that's "in style." Expensive purses and high heels are a must-have if you're ever stepping out. Your hair needs to be flawless at all times. So, to compensate for lack of confidence, or trying the whole "look good, feel good" approach, Black people spend their dollars on looking good. This is some ignorant behavior that needs to be taken out of this culture because you need to crawl before you walk."

That blog had many valid points, and the topic needed

to be addressed. Not too long ago, I was watching an interview of Dapper Dan, an American high-fashion designer. During the interview, they mentioned how Black culture are influencers. One of the points was that we make brands hot, and we like what other people can't have. That's why a lot of people purchase name-brand clothing. They buy these things because they are limited. In large part, we consume these things because of what the brand represents—money. The problem lies when we are so obsessed with looking like money than actually having it. Sadly, reality TV shows and rap music don't influence the community for the better.

There was a film made back in 1954 to educate merchants on the spending habits of Black Americans entitled *The Secret of Selling the Black Negro*. I encourage you to look it up on YouTube. Johnson Publishing Company, who is also the publisher of *Ebony Magazine*, financed the film. The film urged advertisers to promote their products and services in the African American media, pointing out the opinions of others influences Blacks—what their friends think of a particular item often determines whether the sale is made. This is not to say whites don't spend money on fashion, too. It's just that their efforts are more to make sure they look presentable to potential clients and employers. They couldn't care less about being made fun of for how they are dressed on their off workday.

Compared to all consumers, according to Nielson Company, Black people as a group spend thirty percent more of their total income, even though we make $20,000 less than the average household. Eighty-seven percent of annual retail spending consists of Black consumers. Blacks have little to show for their hard-earned dollars because we are big spenders and small investors. It sounds so cliché, but when you know better, you do better.

Back in 2010, I attended a seminar I heard advertised on the radio about raising private money. When I entered the room, I was the only Black person there, also the youngest. While looking around, I thought to myself, *I'm definitely in the right room.* The trainer, Mr. Ledford, and another presenter made me feel very comfortable. In fact, we all took a picture at the end of the seminar. I remember Mr. Ledford saying, "You're going to be rich." A few months later, I received an email from him, but I thought it was sent to me in error the way it was written. The email stated, "You're receiving this email because you inquired about being a part of our team." Then it detailed the requirements. It also said they would select seven people for the team, and anyone chosen would be challenged to earn seven figures in seven years. To be picked, you had to submit an essay about why you wanted to be on the team. Two multimillionaires would review the essay entries. I replied, expressing that I thought the email had been sent to me in error, but I was up for the challenge. He sent an email back telling me to send in my essay.

So, I submitted my essay, and a few weeks later, I received an email informing me that I was one of the seven people chosen. I was elated! At our first meeting, I noticed again that I was the only Black person and the youngest. I was picked along with some other highly successful people. Before working together, we had to sign a few legal confidentiality documents. Mr. Ledford was the head of our group and was big on wealth accumulation.

One thing I noticed while attending these meetings was the vehicles and attire of the other members. My car was newer than most, and my clothing was way more stylish. I had a few knock-off designer bags and shoes during that time—all to look like I had money. When in actuality, I had a mountain of debt and was living paycheck to paycheck. While going over our financial game plans, I learned they had their stuff together, but they looked broke. I remember him telling us to save $10,000 and start clearing our debt. *How in the world am I going to do that?* I thought, not wanting to be the weakest link of the team.

One day, Mr. Ledford came in on a tangent, drilling into us about our progress and finances. We had to detail our budgets and discuss a plan. Through previous conversations, he knew I loved heels. Well, that day, he looked at me and said, "How many pairs of feet do you have?" He then went on to say, "You guys have to be willing to pay the price to be successful." That was my first time hearing that phrase. He told us to watch what we spent so we could invest our money instead of spending it frivolously.

I learned so much during that time, but it was a message I wasn't completely ready to receive. I was still immature in my thinking back then, but it all makes sense now. Unfortunately, the group ended up dissolving because of the lingering effects of the recession, and Mr. Ledford felt our progress in accomplishing our goal was out of reach. So, he stepped down. Back then, my mindset was on spending money to appear like I had it all together. Now I understand what Mr. Ledford was trying to drill into us, and for that, I am forever grateful we crossed paths.

GROUP ECONOMICS

It is important as a community to exercise our buying power and spend responsibly. We have to understand the power we truly possess. Aforementioned, we have $1.2 trillion in buying power, and Blacks are the only culture that does not practice Group Economics to get ahead to capitalize on our buying power.

First, let's define Group Economics. It is one group of

people who agree to actively and consciously pursue a common economic interest to create a sustainable economy for themselves. The Jewish, Italian, and Asian communities have been practicing this principle for ages. In fact, there's a system the Koreans use called Keh. It is an informal lending system where a community contributes a sum of money into a pool, which is then loaned to a single person or family to help them get on their feet. Everyone who contributes to the system receives the pool at some point throughout the lending cycle, and it never ends. There are many different names for these systems, but they all work the same.

Group Economics isn't new. It's a form of self-preservation. Group Economics was used very successfully in many areas—one of which was the Black Wall Street right here in North Carolina. In Durham, during the 1890s-1920s, black businesses flourished, creating a vibrant American middle-class. This was referred to as the Hayti community, named after Haiti—the first free, independent black republic in the western hemisphere. James E. Shepard, Aaron McDuffie Moore, John E. Shepard, and Charles Clinton Spaulding were some of the founding fathers of the growing neighborhood. Shepard, Moore, and Merrick went on to found North Carolina Mutual Life Insurance Co., which became the wealthiest black-owned company during that time. By the early 1900s, Hayti was the first black community to become fully self-sufficient. There were well over 200 businesses, including Lincoln Hospital staffed with black doctors and nurses, a theater, library, and hotels.

So how can we participate in Group Economics? Here are a few ways:

- Start a business
- Support black-owned businesses
- Hire black workers
- Join a community investment group
- Buy real estate
- Become financially literate

I've personally contributed in several ways. As a culture, we have to stop making excuses and make things happen.

June of 2017, I decided to step out of my comfort zone to accelerate my wealth-creating phase. For the first time in my life, and well into my 30's, I decided to get a roommate. I remember making a general status on Facebook asking my friends if they would room with someone temporarily to pay off debt. The majority commented they would. The reason I posed the question was to see what people would do in terms of sacrificing. Little did I know a few months later that I would do it to attain financial freedom and create wealth. I have always enjoyed my peace and having my own space. My living quarters are my sanctuary. One thing to note about me, though, is that I'm all for sacrificing temporarily to reach my goals. And I'm always up for a good challenge.

As I read over the comments on my Facebook post, a few people stated how they put that extra money to good use. Some paid off student loans; others were able to clear debt and start businesses. That was impressive to me. The topic allowed me to think outside the box. The thought of living nearly mortgage-free sounded appealing. Besides, I have a two-story, three-bed, 2-½-bath home, and it's just me. My other rooms are for guests, but I didn't have guests often. My mindset shifted after I calculated the income potential; my mind was made up.

One evening, I came across a website where I wanted to post my listing. I had received a few messages from females and decided to start the interview process. I met with one young lady at a Starbucks, and we both asked questions to see if we would be a good fit. After the interview, I agreed to move forward.

So here I was about to exchange my privacy for cash flow. I'm picky about my space, and clutter gets on my nerves. Not to mention, I'm a serious neat freak. So, I knew this was going to test me.

The day she moved in, she immediately started

cleaning her space and the guest bathrooms. My house was already clean, but I appreciated the fact that she did that. She had plug-ins and all. Not only did she clean her area, as per the contract, she also cleaned the rest of the house like it was hers. This was perfect! I loved it! She was tidy, professional, and paid her rent on time. And get this—she was from South Carolina and had a contracted job here in North Carolina, so she only needed to stay during the week. Therefore, I had my whole house to myself on the weekends.

I was very pleased with my first roommate experience. We became good friends and still are to this day. She only stayed a few months because she ended up accepting another job closer to her home. It took me a short time to get used to sharing my home, but I soon realized it wasn't so bad after all.

After she moved out, I decided to find another roommate. I placed an ad and met with another female. Initially, I had reservations about her cleanliness, but I decided to give it a try. Needless to say, this second one did not work; my initial thoughts about her were correct. Good thing I had her sign a month-to-month rental agreement. I decided to implement that just in case I wanted my space back or things didn't work out. I remember calling my first roommate and telling her that she had set the standard pretty high. We both laughed. I soon realized everyone's definition of clean isn't the same as mine. Not letting the experience discourage me, I gave her the allotted time to find another place to live and placed another ad.

During this next round of selecting, two females inquired. I had already agreed to one of them, and the other female had a deadline to move out of her current place. I started thinking about the income potential of renting two rooms and realized I could live mortgage-free. That sealed the deal for me. Several people tried to talk me out of having two roommates, saying three is a crowd.

At the time, my other guestroom was my office. It had my computer desk and a daybed in it. After advising the other female that we could move forward, I called one of my guy friends over to help me rearrange some things. I decided to turn my dining room into my office. Besides, it was just a room with beautiful furniture. It's not like I would sit down to eat in that area. So, I purchased a chest of drawers to match the daybed, and the second room was all set to rent.

I remembered thinking my home had two rooms that I didn't use. Why not turn them into income streams, or at least temporarily? The house was built with three bedrooms, so obviously three isn't a crowd. For the most part, everyone stayed in their rooms. They hardly ever sat downstairs in the living area. Needless to say, I adapted to having two roommates just fine, so I decided to continue renting out both rooms. And when those deposits hit every month, it made it all worth it.

I'm living mortgage-free, and I love it. At the same time, I'm helping other women save towards their goals. My current roommates are both saving up to purchase their own homes. The income I make from my primary job and side business is now going towards my strategy to create wealth. This is an example of temporary sacrifices for long-term gain. Don't be afraid to step out of your comfort zone in order to put yourself in a better position. If you're single, this may be something you want to consider. Even if you're not single, you can still get creative with renting out your space. Maybe list your property on the Airbnb website for when you're going to be away on vacation, or maybe turn your basement into a room you can rent out.

I could have easily picked up another job for additional income, but right now, I have passive income that I receive without doing any work. Now, my time is freed up to work on my side business. For me, it was a matter of what I wanted the most. Did I want my privacy, or did I want to accelerate my wealth plan? It was a no-brainer. Do I get irritated some days? Yes, but I keep my WHY in perspective.

Years ago, I wanted to turn my extra room into a closet, as if the walk-in closet I have now wasn't enough. It certainly is, but I wanted a big room/closet like someone I saw on social media. Red bottom heels filled the person's closet. (If you are interested in seeing what I'm referring to, do a Google search for StilettoMeUp Shoe Closet.) I looked at her closet dreamy-eyed, thinking how I planned to incorporate something like that in my home. I was still in debt at that time, and my priorities were all out of whack. As I matured, I realized material possessions didn't mean that much to me. My mind shifted from wanting to convert that second room into a shoe closet to using it for a second stream of income. Now, I currently live off of 16% of my income.

Participating in Group Economics has allowed me to accelerate my goals and invest in my education around wealth creation. Keep in mind this is done with a plan. Sometimes you have to live like no one else now so you can live like no one else later.

I've also witnessed this in the Hispanic culture. Many people may laugh and joke about them piled up in a house or car, but guess what? Their median value of family net worth is high than that of Blacks.

There are many ways we can take advantage of Group Economics. It's time for us to think in terms of economic development and determination. A form of predatory economics is happening, and it's destroying Blacks. We must begin to pursue cooperative measures in which we control our communities if we want to get ahead.

<u>CASH VS. CREDIT</u>

There's a great debate about cash and credit. Some say you should preserve your cash and use credit; others tell you to use your cash and not go into debt. Cash and credit are nothing more than tools used for a specific purpose. Too much of anything that is misused can be a bad thing. Truthfully, you can make either work. It all boils down to how knowledgeable you are regarding the risk associated with each. What I know to be true is that you can misuse credit, end up in debt, and get a bad credit rating. You can also misuse cash, resulting in you being broke and living paycheck to paycheck. So, financial literacy is an important factor in determining your outcome.

Let's discuss cash. Having liquid cash can be less stressful than being buried under a mountain of debt. You also don't have to worry about dishing out extra money for interest and late fees when paying with cash. So, from an emotional and psychological standpoint, money allows you to be more in control over your financial future.

The first thing we discussed with having a financial game plan was creating a budget. It's important to have a spending plan for your money. We also know you need to free up income, secure an emergency fund, and clear your consumer debt as quickly as possible. By operating in this format, you can position yourself to make your money work for you. The key is getting out of the cycle of living paycheck to paycheck and start creating financial freedom. Your income is your biggest wealth-building tool, and if you squander it, it can't do much for you.

Once you reach the position where you have money saved and freed up, you can get creative with your ability to invest. Cash provides stability and a foundation for creating more opportunities. I do want to point out here that saving money just for the sake of saving money isn't ideal. You will want to invest it, and here's why.

When saving money, you'll have to take into account inflation. Inflation is a silent killer of your financial freedom plan. In short, inflation is the increase of prices for goods and services in the economy. You will need more money tomorrow to buy the same things you buy today. On average, the inflation rate is at around 2-4% annually, while the average savings account rate is approximately 0.26%. So, you know now that the interest paid on your money doesn't keep up with the rate of inflation. There are a few banks and credit unions that offer rates that will outperform the rate of inflation. Check out the website Magnifymoney.com for the best rates. You can't avoid the impact of inflation, but you can make your money work better for you. Invest your money in vehicles such as a 401(k) or IRA for long-term and short-term. You can also invest in a high-yield certificate of deposit, stocks, and real estate. We'll discuss how to use your cash for real estate in the upcoming chapter.

When I saw my grandmother cut up her credit cards, I stayed away from credit for most of my adult years. When I did finally start using credit cards, I found myself in debt because of the economy. I had good intentions to pay it off, but life happened. The feeling of having that debt lingering was too much for me. All of my cash was tied up paying off debt, and I had no room to invest. Looking back on things now, I should have had an emergency fund secured. The use of credit in that instance was necessary but stressful at the same time.

Aforementioned, credit is a tool, but if you have poor spending habits and lack good money management skills, this can be detrimental to your future. However, if used correctly, credit isn't a bad thing. There are certain reasons why you want to use credit. For example, several establishments will require you to have a good credit score, like when renting an apartment, buying a home, or shopping around for auto insurance with a lower rate. In such cases, you will have to utilize credit to build a credit history. The key here is to manage the debt you have. Let's discuss the factors that make up your credit score:

1. **Payment history: (35%)** – Your account payment information, including any delinquencies and public records. The first thing lenders want to know is whether you have paid your past credit accounts on time.

2. **Credit utilization: (30%)** – This is the total of how much you owe on your accounts. Credit utilization should be less than 30% of your total debts. If you are using a lot of your available credit, this may indicate you are overextended.

3. **Length of credit history: (15%)** – How long ago you opened the accounts and the time since account activity. A longer credit history will increase your score.

4. **New credit: (10%)** – Your pursuit of new credit, including credit card inquires and the number of accounts you have open. Opening several accounts in a short amount of time represents greater risk.

5. **Credit mix: (10%)** – The mix of accounts you have, such as car loans, credit cards, and mortgages.

For the sake of knowing that certain establishments will want you to have a good credit score, it is important to learn how to manage debt. Do not go into debt acquiring a bunch of depreciating assets. Don't splurge on credit, and don't use credit as an emergency fund. Avoid getting caught up in the debt trap. Debt robs you of your future spending power. If you use credit solely to obtain a good score and not as a crutch or looking at it as free money, you'll be better off. One of the things you can do is set up automatic bill pay with your credit card. Then cut up your credit card to avoid being tempted to use it for anything other than paying your bills, and pay the balance in full each month. This way, you're not adding any unnecessary debt. You are paying for things you would have to pay monthly or annually anyway while also earning cashback bonuses or mileage points depending on the perks associated with using your credit card. Pull your credit report yearly to stay on top of everything. You can obtain a free credit report at Annualcreditreport.com.

One of the benefits of having a good credit history is that it will allow you to leverage your personal credit to obtain business credit. You can then use your business credit to buy assets. Whether you want a business or not, establishing business credit will allow you to buy those same assets without having personal liability. This is a form of asset protection.

When it comes to utilizing these tools to create wealth, having a plan is essential. Cash and credit can both be added to your personal arsenal. They both serve different purposes. Cash can be king, and credit can also be king if used properly.

REAL ESTATE

There are several assets you can add to your wealth-creating arsenal. In this chapter, we'll focus on real estate. Some of the wealthiest people in the world made their fortunes through real estate. However, real estate isn't just for the wealthy. It is a proven way to create income outside your primary job or business and grow lasting wealth.

In 2006, I wanted to learn more about real estate. I figured if I went to school for something, it would be that. I have always had an interest in real estate. A couple of weeks into our training, our professor told us if we wanted to be an investor, we didn't need to take that class. He broke down how agents were held liable for many things because of the regulations an investor didn't have to worry about. I was intrigued at that point. After he mentioned this, I discontinued the class and decided to delve into the investing side of things. However, I still had my books to keep me abreast of the things concerning being a real estate agent. I thought the only way to make money in real estate was by becoming an agent.

Back in 2010, I visited the Real Estate Investors Association, also known as REIA. This is where you go to gain knowledge and network with other investors. You can find a local REIA in any city. This was perfect for me. Besides, I had discontinued my enrollment as an agent. Our local REIA was about $20 per visit or $99 for a membership at that time.

I met many experienced individuals within the REIA, and there were a lot of good topics. The only issue I had was the topics were random. They didn't teach investing in order; you had to piece together what you were learning. The networking part was cool. I spoke with a gentleman and his girlfriend about their position in real estate. I asked him what is it that he did, and he explained he wholesaled real estate. He gave me a brief overview, stating he made $5,000 on his last deal. He also advised that he didn't use any of his own money or credit. At this point, I was even more intrigued.

He told me that he found the deal and gave it to an investor for a middleman fee. This seemed like something I could handle. All I had to do was find the property, find an investor, and add my fee. Well, I quickly learned it was a little more detailed than that.

During another REIA meeting, I met a local landlord who stated he was looking for properties and gave me his business card. I also collected a few other cards of investors and real estate agents. I had made up my mind that I was going to jump in and try to wholesale.

One evening, I met up with two investors at a local Borders Bookstore to talk about deals. One of the investors told me that he had a property he was trying to sell. I thought to myself, *Well, I'm halfway to my middleman fee.*

Later that evening, I pulled out my business cards to call the landlord. I told him that I had a property he could look at and asked if he could meet. We agreed to meet at a designated time. Upon arriving at the house, we noticed it had been remodeled. The landlord looked around and said the home looked nice. After that, I can't tell you what happened. I didn't have the proper contracts or anything. I knew nothing about analyzing the deal or anything.

After that ordeal, I realized I needed help. Wanting to have a mentor to assist me, I reached out to a gentleman over the REIA at that time, but he was too busy. I'm a very structured person and not having a step-by-step guide frustrates me. At this point, I decided to put real estate on hold.

Fast forward to November 2012. I attended a millionaire mind training. This was a three-day training that had a lot of great information. The event touched on investing and tax liens. That was my first time hearing about purchasing tax liens, and I was very interested in that, as well. I took notes so I could research it at a later time. During this training, I also met three guys—one of which was named Dr. Joe White. Joe explained he was in real estate amongst having other businesses. Because I was interested in learning more about this area, we exchanged phone numbers.

A couple of months later, Joe and I agreed to meet up to discuss business. At this stage in my life, I was all over the place. I was still at my corporate job and involved in two network marketing companies—one of which my supervisors introduced me to. She also told me about a book that would soon change the trajectory of my life. The book is titled *Rich Dad Poor Dad*, and it is by far one of my favorites. The book broke down what was called the Cashflow Quadrant. This quadrant explained the difference in how wealth was created and the tax advantages and disadvantages. It also compared the Employee and Self-employed Quadrant against the Investor and Big Business Quadrant, noting the importance of leveraging your time.

I vividly recall telling Joe that I had those businesses and even tried to recruit him. Thinking back on that, it was hilarious. Joe looked at me and told me that I had to focus on one thing. He saw I had too much going on and hadn't mastered anything. I heard him, but I wasn't listening; I wasn't ready to hear his message. He also told me that he could mentor me with business, but at that time, I was still living paycheck to paycheck and couldn't afford the mentorship investment every month. Even though I couldn't hire him as my mentor, he and I became good friends and shared a lot of our goals with each other.

When I had my "ah-ha" moment back in 2013, I started sharing my story, and when I realized there was a need for help, I started honing in on my personal financial education platform. I curated self-paced courses, provided one-on-one coaching, and created several eBooks. I completely dedicated myself to my brand and to helping others. Joe noticed my progress and gave great feedback.

He had courses, as well. One course, in particular, was the missing link to what I needed in the beginning when I first started trying to get into real estate. Joe had his own wholesaling course! Look at how this came right back to me.

Because I knew Joe had this course and seeing his success, I would refer a lot of clients to his platform as a way for them to make extra money. By doing this, I was also adding value to Joe. One day, he sent me a link to his course and told me that I could access it for free! I tell you, the stars aligned perfectly. I now had a guide to follow and a mentor.

Now, I was invested in my brand—doing speaking engagements, upgrading systems, creating blogs, etc. I didn't have the time to focus solely on real estate. My income was increasing, so I wasn't in a rush to get back into real estate. That would soon change, though.

In 2017, real estate presented itself to me again. It was like the universe was telling me to pay attention. This time around, it was for tax lien investing. I saw the potential profits that I could make and decided to invest my money in it. I decided to go back and take the wholesale course, as well. After reviewing the income potential, a light bulb went off for me to focus primarily on real estate and have that replace my primary job income, accelerate my retirement, and allow the financial freedom I longed for.

As I started focusing on real estate more, I began noticing younger individuals excelling in it. I came across an article about a young lady who retired from her nine-to-five job at thirty-two years old. That sealed the deal for me.

I quickly had an idea to rebrand my business to incorporate real estate with my personal finance brand, and my target audience was corporate women. I wanted to show them how to create wealth while working a nine-to-five by actively and passively investing in real estate. This allowed me to talk about finance and real estate simultaneously. The rewards I received in such a short period proved why real estate kept coming back to me. Now, I'm kicking myself for not sticking with it when I first started.

I committed myself to following successful people in real estate and indulged in a lot of podcasts, YouTube videos, webinars, and events. I became obsessed with it. Not only was I equipped with the knowledge, but I also backed that with action, and within seven months of doing real estate part-time, I surpassed what I had made full-time to date. The information I have gained has allowed me to position myself to accelerate my financial freedom date. I consider that date as the day my assets will cover my basic needs. So, my goal is to have income-producing assets to pay for my lifestyle. That's the Holy Grail.

THE REAL ESTATE GAME

As profitable as it can be to get into real estate, not everyone knows how to get started. I can tell you now that this has already been a life-changing transition for me. There are many creative ways to make money in real estate. No wonder real estate has afforded so many individuals financial freedom. I'm going to share with you a few ways.

There indeed may come a time in your life when you'll want to start creating wealth by buying real estate. If you are just starting out, flipping a house may be an ideal way. There are three ways you can flip a house. The following are the technical terms:

- The first method is known as **retailing**. This is when you buy a house in bad shape, do repairs to fix it up, then turn around and sell it.
- The second way you can flip a house is through **wholesaling**. Wholesaling involves finding a home for sale, buying it, and flipping it to an investor as is for a fast profit.
- The third way to flip a house is by **assigning** the contract to purchase. Using this method, you'll commit to buying the house. Instead of closing the deal yourself, you assign it to a real estate investor—for a fee, of course. The investors will take over and complete the purchase themselves.

Within the real estate community, you will often hear the word wholesaling. Many courses, podcasts, and YouTube videos mention wholesaling. So, from here on out, we will use the term wholesaling.

Wholesaling real estate is beneficial if you want to get into real estate but don't have much cash. You can do this without using your credit. Here are a few quick steps on how to wholesale:

1. **Find distressed properties or motivated sellers.** Distressed properties are great because the owners aren't too attached emotionally to them, and therefore, the property can be purchased under market value. In other words, you are buying at a discount. You can find these properties by simply driving around your neighborhood. Look for homes where there may be high grass, boarded-up windows, code violation notices on the door, or other signs of abandonment. You can also find homes listed on free sites like Craigslist, Facebook Marketplace, and Zillow, to name a few. Motivator sellers are sellers who are in desperate need of selling their homes. For example, they may be facing foreclosure or have inherited a property they don't want. My top two ways for finding deals are distressed properties and tax-delinquent owners.

2. **Make an offer.** Once you have found a property, you will have to determine if it's a good deal. I use the following formula to determine if something is a good deal in my area: *After Repair Value (ARV) x 70% – Repairs – My Fee = Maximum Allowable Offer (MAO)*. You can look up how to determine the ARV on YouTube or ask a realtor. In short, the ARV is the amount the house is worth if it is in perfect condition. The number is determined by the price of the most recent homes sold similar to your property.

FYI – The investors are looking to purchase a property at a discount. They want to make sure that they can sell the property for a nice profit after they fix it. If you're not sure what repairs are needed for the house, you can leave that to be determined by the investor or reach out to a contractor. When presenting your offer to the seller, you'll want to start at a number below your MAO. Once they agree, have them sign your contract. You can use the help of an investor-friendly attorney, a title company, or a real estate agent to get a contract. Or ask others who are doing this in your area. Most people that wholesale use a generic real estate purchase agreement.

As far as finding the owners, you will use a method called skip tracing. This is when you pull data to locate the owner's contact information. You can find numbers on free websites such as Truepeoplesearch.com or use Fiverr.com for a cost-effective way of searching. As you start building capital, you can use more expensive ways to search for the owner's contact information.

3. **Find a title company or investor-friendly attorney.** Depending on your state, you'll use either a title company or an attorney to handle your transactions. An investor-friendly attorney is knowledgeable of how to handle assignment closings.

4. **Find a buyer.** Cost-effective ways to find buyers include advertising the contract for sale on free websites like Zillow, Craigslist, and Facebook Marketplace. Network with others in real estate. Also, look up your local REIA and attend those meetings.

5. **Negotiate with the buyer.** Take a look at the formula in action:

$90k (ARV) x 70% (Discount) − $15k (Repairs) − $5k (Assignment fee) = $43k (MAO)

I lock the contract up for $43k or under with the seller. Let's say I lock it up at $43k exactly. I would then add

$43k plus my fee of $5k, which is $48k to present to my end buyer. I would start higher than $48k because the buyer will also want to negotiate for a better price. Anything you get over what you have under contract with the seller is a profit. Once agreed, you'll sign an assignment contract with the buyer.

6. **Close the deal.** Submit the contracts to the attorney or title company. The closing company will set a date to close. You pick up your check.

These are some quick steps to wholesaling. It may seem like a lot, but once you get through a couple, it will be like second nature to you. It's not hard at all. However, this method will require your time. Even if you work this part-time, you can still make a good source of income. Wholesaling is like an ATM or a high-paying job. This is a way you can build up your capital in real estate. In turn, you take that capital and invest it into passive income streams.

One thing I love about wholesaling is that there's no risk. You can get started with little to no money or credit. I still remember my very first deal. I made it a goal to get 60 properties that weekend. After filling up my gas tank, I rode around different areas and found a house with fire damage. Once I contacted the landlord, I learned they wanted to sell the property. I locked up this deal in one week and made $6,198.50. All it took was gas money and some of my time.

If you want to get started now, begin by indulging in everything real estate. Join Facebook groups. I have one called the Creating Wealth Society. Join your local REIA. I have a course on this at www.creatingwealthsociety.com.

WHOLESALING

Wholesaling properties is a great entry point to real estate and can be very lucrative. This has changed my life in a short time. If you're open to committing to this strategy, I'm sure you'll say the same.

NOTE: Wholesaling is legal for the most part. At the time of this writing, Illinois recently made it illegal to wholesale without a license. A solution is to go ahead and get your license, or you can use transactional funding to do a double close. There are courses on Groupon where you can get your license at a very reasonable rate. You can also learn how to do wholesaling virtually in other states as an alternative.

Passive Income

Rental property investments can be highly profitable when the right decisions are made. Just like the game Monopoly, investing in real estate to create wealth is a process that begins with just one single property and grows. To make a rental property purchase successful, you must find a bargain. Remember our formula from the wholesaling example. Pay no more than 70%-80% of the home's value.

You can start with wholesaling to build your capital and get your feet wet. Then you can use that capital to purchase or put down money on your own rental. Let's say you had $40k cash and bought one property. The property is worth $50k and is rented for $500 per month. You can refinance with the bank for 80% percent of the home's market value. At this point, the bank would give you back what you put in. Now your tenant is the one paying down the loan. In this example, you will roughly make about $50 in positive cash flow or passive income per month. Now, you'll rinse and repeat.

Tax Lien Investing

There is a way of getting real estate exposure in your portfolio without investing in a property; it is through tax lien certificates. As an investor, you can buy liens in an auction, paying the amount of taxes owed in return for the right to collect back your initial investment plus interest payment from the property owner. This is a great way to stay ahead of inflation. The interest rates vary depending on the jurisdiction or the state. Iowa has a rate of 24%, being one of the highest.

So, how do tax liens work? When a property owner fails to pay their property tax bill, a lien is placed against the property. The government then sells the tax lien certificate to the investors in order to recover the delinquent amount due to them. The property owner has a certain amount of time to pay back the taxes and penalties, known as the redemption period. If they fail to pay, you, as the lienholder, can initiate foreclosure proceedings to take ownership of the property. However, if the owner comes back to pay, you will get your money back plus interest. This is what makes tax liens an attractive investment. Of course, you will need up-front costs to take advantage of this strategy. However, investing in tax liens offers much lower capital requirements when compared to other forms of investing. You can start investing for as little as a couple of hundred dollars. This is a great strategy to use to get more interest on your money. Tax lien investing can be a good way to see a 12-34% return on your investment.

Why is this a win-win for you? You can profit in two ways with tax lien investing: through interest payments or taking ownership of the property.

Financial Freedom

There was a great quote by Robert Kiyosaki that said, "More important than the how we achieve financial freedom, is the why. Find your reasons why you want to be free and wealthy." On your journey towards financial freedom, it's necessary to understand your WHY. Your WHY is going to keep you accountable when you feel like giving up. Anyone can start something, but not everyone can finish what they set out to do. One thing true about successful people is that they succeed because they are clear on their WHY.

Let's talk about what is your WHY exactly. Your Why is nothing more than a deeper purpose or mission. It's the reason you do the things you do. For instance, it may be to provide something for your family or a greater cause. Many believe money is their Why, but in reality, money is a tool and not a purpose or goal. You may want more money to obtain a certain outcome or acquire a specific thing.

For this reason, your Why has to be deeper than just to "get money." For example, my Why is to have the freedom to live life on my terms. Less stress and less worrying about finances. I'm positioning myself to have enough passive income to cover my lifestyle. I don't have a desire to swap time for dollars. Time is your most valuable asset, so we have to consider how we're using it and if what we're doing makes sense. For me, it's also the freedom to wake up when I want, spend more time with family members, travel the world, and give back and help more people on a granular scale.

"Real wealth is about freedom."
– James Clear

Money gives you many options, and financial freedom is one of them. To obtain true financial freedom, we ultimately want to reach a point where our money works for us, which is the basic concept for achieving financial freedom. For some of us, we have been taught we must continuously work hard for the things we want. We were not taught to have our money work for us so we could buy back our time. In my opinion, there's no greater feeling than being free with time—not having to work by force, but by choice, and having the ability to experience life and all that it truly has to offer. That's the power you have over your life when financial freedom is obtained. Being trapped in a linear cycle keeps us enslaved to a dollar and a system, limiting our time.

At this point, before we go any further, establish what your Why is. Once you have determined that, it's time to implement a plan to reach financial freedom. One of the first things to do is accept responsibility and own up to your past financial mistakes. By doing so, you can reset and learn from those mistakes to increase your financial IQ and shift your mindset to reach your goals.

We can't discuss financial freedom without discussing finances. This topic is very important; yet, we refuse to educate ourselves on it properly. When it comes to finances, we have to properly manage our income, savings, and investments. "Make money, manage money, and multiply money" is a phrase I used when coaching my students. Making money isn't enough. My mother used to say, "A fool and his money will soon part." If you don't know how to manage the money you have, you'll squander it. The challenge most people face is they allow money to control them. If you don't track your income and spending, you can't track when you will become financially free. In short, create a budget, tackle personal debts, and invest. Refer back to the previous chapter about overcoming financial challenges for the steps you need to take.

Besides learning how to manage your money, you'll want to set some goals. Having actionable steps is going to keep you on your game. When thinking about your goals, have a target financial freedom number. What does this number look like for you? You are technically financially free when your passive income is enough to cover your living expenses. It's that simple. I remember posing a question to the ladies in my Facebook community about how much money they needed to quit their jobs. The numbers they mentioned were extremely high. The truth is, you don't need nearly as much income as you think to survive and live a good life. If you are currently employed or self-employed, how much money do you need to cover your bills? This is a way to reverse engineer your way to your goal.

I would even go as far as to say this can also be a retirement number. Let's give an example. If I needed $3k to cover my bills and necessities monthly, I would focus on getting a certain number of properties that can cash-flow what I need monthly. So, if my goal is to net about $500 per property, I need six houses on the board. I now have a goal of getting those six houses as quickly as possible. Remember earlier when I explained how to get started in real estate? You can use that to start. To take this a step further, you can maximize the amount of income you receive by renting out shared rooms. It would limit the number of houses needed because you can maximize your revenue by rooms rented. Sound pretty simple, right? You don't need $50k a month to quit your job or be financially free—unless for some odd reason you have astronomical bills and debts that exceed that amount. You can reach your financial freedom goal sooner than you think.

There are two different mentalities when it comes to achieving financial freedom: a wealth mentality and a poverty mentality. Those with the wealth mentality are proactive and plan for future obligations while understanding every dollar has a major role in hitting their target. In contrast, those with a poverty mentality tend to be more reactive. Instead of being financially prepared, they attack issues as they arise. Many people who have this mentality work just to pay bills and do not properly save or invest until they have more money. Which mentality are you choosing to adopt?

There couldn't be more of a perfect time to shift your mindset and start working towards your financial freedom roadmap. All of the rules to financial freedom and wealth-building are out there and easily accessible. With a well-conceived plan of action, you can decide on your destination and identify the steps to get there. Otherwise, you will be chasing your tail, living paycheck to paycheck.

Until this point, the environments we grew up in have had a significant effect on the person we are today. I'm personally thankful for the environment where I grew up. Without it, I may not have been as motivated to break generational curses, which would ultimately liberate me so I can liberate others. Our parents did the best they could, given the information they had. Sometimes you don't know what you don't know. Despite your financial situation today, you have complete power to start making better choices to overcome the inevitable results from the lack of education.

Positioning yourself to reach true financial freedom can yield many benefits—not just for your personal gain, but for the lives you can touch. There is someone out there who is counting on you to overcome your challenges so you can liberate them.

The dash that is placed in-between the dates when you were born and when you expire is what you make it. Learn how to overcome the many lessons that life, aka Earth School, is designed to teach you, because if you don't, you will continue to repeat each lesson until you have passed the test.

I'll leave you with one last quote:

"Financial freedom my only hope,
"F" livin' rich and dyin' broke."– Jay Z

WHAT LEGACY WILL YOU LEAVE BEHIND?

About the Author

Andrel Harris is the founder of the Creating Wealth Society. In addition, she is a Certified Financial Educator, Financial Literacy Advocate & Coach, and Real Estate Investor.

Andrel's mission is to educate and empower corporate women on the importance of financial literacy by helping them leverage their current resources to build a solid financial foundation and create wealth by investing in real estate—both actively and passively. Andrel specializes in delivering financial education, economic empowerment, and brand development through seminars, online courses, and personal coaching. To date, she has spent over a decade working in the financial industry. She has helped numerous people regain financial control and start investing. Because of her discipline and accomplishments, Andrel has been featured in the prestigious *Forbes Magazine*.

CPSIA information can be obtained
at www.ICGtesting.com
Printed in the USA
LVHW050759170623
750059LV00055B/1159